INTERNAL MIGRATION and SOCIO-ECONOMIC DEVELOPMENT

N R PRABHAKARA

Publisher's Name: West Harmony Productions

PREFACE

Internal migration is a important element of population redistribution and equilibrium. The purpose of this work is to explain the changing patterns of internal migration in India over the period 1971 to 2001. Further, an attempt has been made to find out the various determinants causing the changing patterns of migration. The rate of migration among major states of India in last two decades were determined. In all the four censuses, rural-rural migration was found the dominant migration steam in India. Employment for males and marriage for female were found to be the main reason for migration respectively. Maharashtra and Madya Pradesh lead among all in-migrating states, Uttar Pradesh and Bihar occupied top place among out-migrating states.

This multidisciplinary comparative study of internal migration in several regions of the world is the combination of several years' collaboration by leading anthropologists, demographers, economists, and sociologists. It fills a gap in the migration literature by providing the opportunity for scholars in these fields to ask new questions and give new answers to the key problems in the study of internal migration, in a comparative context, and to address the problems in regions of varying levels of economic development, and with different economic systems. Despite high rate of internal migration, India is urbanizing relatively slowly.

The problem of migration is a prime example of a subject that requires the skills and approaches of scholars from several disciplines; neither the questions that must be asked nor the methods of analysis required to answer them are within the province of any single discipline. Migration statistics are used primarily to study demographic trends and their economic and social relationships.

Emigration of people from the rural areas to the cities has been a major factor of socio-economic change in developing societies. If on the one hand, emigration has acted as a feeder to urban growth, it has on the other, played an important role in the modernization and development of the rural areas. From both points of view the study of emigration assumes a special significance for sociologists. Although this work is only an attempt to investigate the social and economic consequences of migration in Karnataka state (India), the findings of this work can be generalized, safely, for the rest of the countryside as well.

The present study examines the relationship between population change and migration with emphasis on the changes that occur in the population redistribution. It has been generally accepted that the cause-effect relationship between population change and migration can go in either direction. That is, population change once generated has significant influence on the migration and vice-verse. That they are mutually interdependent and interacting hardly needs to be emphasized. There is need to understand the nature of these changes, and there is even greater need to un reveal the casual interrelations, if any.

Migration is a basic social process. As Durkheim has shown, in the early stages of social growth, it has been the foremost factor in the division of labor and specialization of functions. In fact, for migration, societies would have hardly attained the complex form of organization they have attained today.

N. R. PRABHAKARA　　　　　　　October 18, 2025

Acknowledgement

I would like to extend my regards to my mother Late. N Nagamma, who made me to reach to this point in my life.

My thanks to my brother- in-law K V Jayasimha and my sister-in-law Rama Jayasimha, who helped me unconditionally in my D Lit work.

Finaly it is my family. My sincere thanks to my wife Padma Latha who helped me in my work. My heart felt thanks to my son Mohan Ram, my daughter-in-law Preeti Ram and finally my grandson Vishva Ram.

Finaly I extend my thanks to every one who helped me in my life.

Statement of The Problem

In recent years, several changes in India are likely to have impacted on the pattern and pace of migration. The pattern of growth in the last two decades has steadily widened the gap between agriculture and non-agriculture and between rural and urban areas, and it has steadily concentrated in a few areas and a few states. The growing spatial inequalities in economic opportunities must have necessarily also impacted on the pace and pattern of migration. Uneven growth and a growing differential between agriculture and industry is a necessary condition of the pattern of development. Since migration is diverse, attention has generally been focused on different groups of internal migrants, and a great deal of analysis has focused on the poorest segments, for whom both the cost and benefits could potentially be the highest.

Data on internal migration in India is drawn from two main sources- the Census of India and the quinquennial migration surveys carried out by the National Sample Survey. Census results for migration are available only till 2001, whereas NSS results are available till 2007-2008. Migration is one of the three basic components of population growth of any area. It influences the size, composition and distribution of the population. In the middle of the 20th century volume of inter-state migration in India was low due to predominance of agriculture, rigidity of the caste system, the role of joint families, the diversity of language and culture, food habits and lack of education (Chatterjee and Boss,1997, Nair and Narayan, 1985, Zachariah, 1964). But the rapid transformation of Indian economy, improvement in level of education and that of transport and communication facilities, shift of work force from agriculture to industry and other tertiary activities accelerated mobility among Indian people in recent times.

In the 2001 census, 309 million people were migrants on the

place of last residence, which constitutes about 30 percent of the total population of the country. This number indicates an increase of around 37 percent from 1991 (226 million) and 100 percent since 1971(159 million). Some of the main determinants of migration have been identified as high population density, surplus of labor force, high employment rate, meager incomes, dissatisfaction with housing, demand for higher schooling, rural-urban wage differentials. India has embarked upon the new economic policy in the year 1991-popularly known as liberalization of the Indian economy. The basic features of new economic policy are to reduce governmental expenditure in order to reduce fiscal deficit, opening up of the economy for export-oriented growth, removal of governmental control and licensing and encouraging private participation for competition and efficiency. Both the supporters and critiques of new economic policy believed that economic reforms would increase internal migration.

The proponents believed that the new impetus would boost economy and job opportunities leading to increased pull factors conducive for accelerated rural to urban migration. On the other hand, the opponents held that economic reforms would adversely affect the village and cottage industries and impoverish rural population leading to increased rural-urban migration (Kundu 1997). Although there was considerable success in achieving economic growth from 2 to 3 per cent of growth in GDP in the pre reform era to over 6 per cent during 1991-2011, its impact on internal migration has not been assessed. The latest census of 2011 throws several interesting results in respect to the internal migration, its regional pattern, and the contribution of rural to urban migration in urban growth (Bhagat and Mohanty 2008).

This work argues that it is not the poor and disadvantaged who are migrating more, but migrants belong largely to better off sections of Indian society. Although migration is emerging an important phenomenon from economic, political, and public health points of views (Bhagat 2008), migration research finds low priority among

Indian Demographers. This is partly because since the early 1990s with a paradigm shift in the demographic research tilting to the issues of reproductive health, the interest in migration research in general and internal migration has dwindled considerably among Indian demographers. This is also reflected in the new datasets namely Demographic Health Surveys- known as National Family Health Surveys (NFHS – An Indian version of DHS), and District Level Health Surveys (DLHS). However, these datasets did not consider migration as an important variable affecting health status in general and reproductive health in particular. On the other hand, the wealth of data available in Indian censuses on migration is grossly neglected by Indian demographers who are busy with data collection exercises funded by external agencies (Bose 2003). Thus, we find very few recent 3demographic studies on India's internal migration and its causes and consequences. This study presents the trends and patterns of internal migration during the last three decades and argues that people belonging to the lowest socio-economic categories are less migratory than otherwise.

In 2001, the Census reported 309 million internal migrants. Of these migrants, 70.7 percent were women. Two thirds of the migrants (67.2 percent) were rural and only 32.8 percent urban. Male migrants were relatively more numerous in the urban stream (53.1 percent of male migrants were urban compared with only 24.4 percent of female migrants) and in more distant streams. The percentage of male migrants in inter-district and inter-state migration was 52.2 percent, 26.7 percent and 21.1 percent, respectively, compared with 66.9 per cent, 23 per cent and 10.1 per cent, respectively, for female migrants in these three streams.

The National Sample Survey (NSS) estimates 326 million migrants in 2007-2008 (28.5 percent of the population). It gives a picture similar to the Census in terms of female predominance, and the relatively higher proportion of male migrants in the urban stream and with increasing distance.

Table 1: Number of migrants and migration rate, 1981-2001.

Census Year	Place of residence	Number of Migrants (in '000)			Migration Rate		
		Person	Male	Female	Person	male	Female
1981	Total	201607	59235	142371	30.0	17.2	44.3
	Rural	143583	31354	112229	28.3	12.1	45.3
	Urban	58024	27881	30143	36.8	33.2	40.8
1991	Total	225888	61134	164754	27.0	14.1	40.9
	Rural	159190	31196	127994	25.6	9.8	42.5
	Urban	66698	29938	36759	31.0	26.3	36.2
2001	Total	309386	90678	218708	30.1	17.0	44.1
	Rural	207774	42529	165245	28.0	11.1	45.8
	Urban	101612	48149	53463	36.5	32.0	39.4

Source: Census of India; Migration Tables, 1981-2001.

According to the Census (Table 1), the migration rate of all segments peaked in 1981 at 30.0 percent, declined in 1991 to 27.0 percent, and increased to 30.1 percent in 2001. Between 1981 and 1991, the total number of migrants grew by only 12 percent, but between 1991 and 2001, the migrant stock increased by 37 percent. However, the successive rounds of the NSS (except the 49th Round, which was also less representative) show an increasing trend in total migration rate since 1983. But the NSS findings are that these trends are mainly due to raising female migration rate both in rural and urban areas.

Internal migration refers to the process of population redistribution within the national boundary of a country. Such movements often involve significant population shift even though the migrants do not cross any international boundary. Evidence indicates a continuous shift of population within a country as a response to a variety of social, economic and demographic factors in both developed and less developed parts of the world. Apart from specific migration waves in different countries, the processes of industrialization and urbanization have provoked significant shift of people from rural to urban areas.

In the less developed parts of the world, another factor that has contributed to this rural-urban migration is the gap in the levels of development between the two areas. In more recent times, the world has witnessed a series of forced internal migration, particularly in Africa, as a result of civil war, ethnic conflict, famine, deteriorating economic conditions and political repression. These instances of internal migration have had significant bearings on the population geography of the individual countries. In the following section, an account of the levels and nature of internal migration in India is presented.

India's urban population was 79 million in 1961 and increased to 377 million in 2011 in a half century. By 2030 it is likely to reach about 600 million (Ahluwalia 2011). The share of in-migrants (all durations of residence) in the population of urban areas has increased from 31.6 percent in 1983 to 33.0 percent in 1999-2001 to 35 percent in 2007-2008, for which the latest data are available from National Sample Survey (NSS). The increase in the migration rate to urban areas has primarily occurred owning to increase in the migration rate for females. Although females migrate on account of marriage, many of them take up work sooner or later, joining the pool of migrant workers in urban areas. On the other hand, the male migration rate in urban areas has remained constant (between 26 and 27 percent), but employment-related reasons of migration for males increased from 42 percent in 1993 to 52 percent in 1999-2000 to 56 percent in 2007-2008 (NSS 2010). This shows the increasing importance of employment related migration to urban areas. When we disaggregate the reason of migration employment related reasons go as high as 62 percent in male rural to urban migration.

Over time, the Census shows an increase in urban migration and in inter-state migration (Table 2). Total urban migration as a percentage of total migration increased from 28.7 percent in 1981 to 29.5 percent in 1991 and further to 32.85 percent in 2001. As a corelate, rural-ward migration declined. However, interpreting 2001 stream-wise results are problematic, because a high percentage of migrants both in rural and in urban areas could not be classified by stream.

Table 2: Percentage distribution of internal migrants in India by different streams 1981-2001.

Census Year	Rural-Rural	Urban-Rural	Unclassified-Rural	Total Rural	Rural-Urban	Urban-Urban	Unclassified-Urban	Total Urban	Total
1981	65.03	6.11	0.08	71.22	16.59	12.1	0.1	28.79	100
1991	64.21	5.97	0.29	70.47	17.67	11.7	0.16	29.53	100
2001	55.51	4.2	7.45	67.16	16.71	11.82	4.32	32.85	100

Source: Census of India, 1981, 1991 and 2001, Table D-2.

The NSS results for the more recent period (1999-2000 to 2007-2008) show that among the total migrants, there was an increase in rural-urban and urban-urban migration streams (NSS Report 533, p. 31). Internal migration spurred primarily by employment and marriage helps shape the economic and social life of the region. About two out of ten Indians are internal migrants who have moved across district or state lines. According to census data released southern states, especially Tamil Nadu and Kerala, have shown the highest increase in migrant population. With 45.36 crore migrants in India, every third citizen of the country is a migrant. Of these, 69 percent are women, majority of whom have cited marriage. Migrants constitute 37.8 of India's 121.03 crore population. Over the last decade, the total number of migrants in India rose by 44.35 percent from 31.45 crore in 2001. During the same period India 's population grew 17.64 percent.

Tamil Nadu's migrant population surged 98 percent from 1.58 crore in 2001 to 3.13 crore in 2011. During the same period, the population of the state grew by 15.6 percent. Migrants now constitute 43.4 percent of the state's population compared to 25.44 percent in 2011. Kerala's migrant population has grown by 77 percent – from 0.92 crore in 2001 to 1.63 crore in 2011. The state's population in the same period grew by 4.9 percent. In Kerala, nearly 49 percent of the population were called migrants as against 28.93 percent in 2001.

Karnataka too has shown a 50 percent increase in its migrant population – from 1.66 crore to 2.50 crore. Only Andhra Pradesh, with a 40 percent rise in migrant population, has shown a growth below the national average – its migrant population increased from 2.34 crore to 3.32 crore during this period.

Table 3: States with high Migrant Growth Rate

States	2001	2011 percent	Growth %	Growth of state population
Tamil Nadu	1.58 cr*	3.13 cr	98%	15.6%
Manipur	0.04 cr	0.07 cr	97%	18.7%
Meghalaya	0.04 cr	0.08 cr	109%	27.8%
Kerala	0.92 cr	1.63 cr	77%	4.9%
J & K	0.18 cr	0.28 cr	55%	23.7%
Assam	0.67 cr	1.02 cr	52%	16.9%
Karnataka	1.66 cr	2.50 cr	51%	15.7%
Andhra Pradesh	2.34 cr	3.32 cr	42%	11.1%
India	31.45 cr	45.36 cr	44%	17.64%

- 1crore= 10 million.

As per the first view, the main cause of rapid urban growth is traced to the increasing pressure of population on farmland in densely populated agrarian economics. Deficiency of reproducible tangible capital relative to labor in the face of a high population density exacerbates the problem of rural unemployment and underemployment, which in turn fosters the rural-urban population movement. The low rate of growth of industrial employment and the high rate of rural-to-urban migration makes for excessive, even explosive urbanization involving a transition from rural unemployment to excessive urban unemployment and underemployment.

Population in the urban areas expands due to the following three factors: natural growth of population, rural to urban migration and reclassification of rural areas as urban in course of time. State-wise data on inter-state migrants by place of birth would help to identify those, which were most preferred destinations. The Table 4 below shows the most important 10 states in terms of inter-state migration, all of which reported more than 1 million in-migrants by place of birth from outside the state, as well as from other countries. This, it may be pointed out, includes both old migrants as well as the recent migrants. Maharashtra is at the top of the list with 7.9 million in-migrant population, followed by Delhi (5.6 million) and West Bengal (5.5 million). The percentage of the in-migrants to the total population in these three states were, 8.2%, 40.8%, 7.0% respectively, accounting for about 39.5% of the total inter-state migrants in the country.

Table 4: Total inter-state migrants by place of birth in major states – INDIA (in '000)

States	Total Population	Total in-migrants	Percent of in-migrants o total population	Share of total migrants
INDIA	1028610	485087	4.7	100.0
Maharashtra	96879	7954	8.2	16.4
Delhi	13851	5646	40.8	11.6
West Bengal	80176	5582	7.0	11.5
Uttar Pradesh	166197	2972	1.8	6.1
Haryana	21145	2952	14.0	6.1
Gujrat	50671	2603	5.1	5.4

Madhya Pradesh	60348	2306	3.8	4.8
Karnataka	52851	2152	4.1	4.4
Punjab	24359	2131	8.7	4.4
Rajasthan	56507	1846	3.3	3.8
Jharkhand	26946	1798	6.7	3.7
Bihar	82999	1794	2.2	3.7
Andhra Pradesh	76201	1052	1.4	2.2
Chhattisgarh	20834	1020	4.9	2.1
Rest	198639	670	3.4	13.8

Source: Table D-1; Census of India, 2001.

Out of the total migrants numbering about 258 million in India who migrated within the state, 17.4 percent were in the age group 15-24 years, 23.2 percent in 25-34 years and 35.6 percent in 35-69 years. Among migrants by place of birth from outside the state of enumeration in India, 36.1 percent were in the age group 35-59 years and 24.7 percent in the age group 25-34 years. This higher proportion in the older and economically active age groups perhaps reflects their migration for work in a new state. The estimated migration rate at All-India level for rural and urban areas in 2007-08 is nearly 29 percent of the persons were migrants with significant rural-urban and male-female differentials. The migration rate in the rural areas (26 percent) was far lower than thew migration rate in urban areas (35 per cent). Moreover, magnitude of male migration rate was far lower than female migration rate, in both the rural and urban areas. In the rural areas nearly 48 per cent of the females were migrants while the male migration rate was only 5 per cent, and in the urban areas, the male migration was nearly 26 per cent compared to female migration rate of 46 per cent. Nominal rural-urban differential was observed for female migration rate.

Table 5: Migration Rate (per 1000 persons) 2007-08.

Category of Person	Rural	Urban	Total
1	2	3	4
Male	54	259	109
Female	477	456	472
Total	261	354	285

The share of different categories of migrants and persons in the country is presented to have an, understanding of the magnitude of migrants in different category of persons. It may be noted that 74 percent of the persons of the country lived in rural areas but the share of rural areas in total migrants were about 67 percent, while the urban areas shared nearly 26 per cent of the persons of the country but shared nearly 33 per cent of the migrants. It is seen that female migrants outnumbered their male counterparts in both the rural and urban areas: rural female shared nearly 36 per cent of the total population but most of the migration in the country were rural females (nearly 60 per cent) and similarly though urban females shared only 13 per cent.[1]

The data has been collected on the place of my last residence to understand the pattern of migration. It is likely that after one moves out of the place of birth, one may continue to migrate from one place to another. The data on migration by last residence in India as per 2001 Census, shows that the number of migrants were 314 million. Out of 314 million migrants by last residence, 268 million migrants (85%) were found to be from within the state. At all India level migrants account for 24.68% of the population. In the case of rural- population the share of migrants is 22.74% where, as the corresponding share in urban population is 30.65%. Among migrants in rural India, male migrants constitute 14.60% and female migrants 85.40%, whereas in urban India, male migrants constitute 41.12% and female migrants 58.88%. Clearly, female migrants have

1 NSS, Report NO. 533; Migration in India, July, 2007, June, 2008.

outnumbered, their male counterparts in both the sectors. Their dominance is more pronounced in rural India than in urban India.

Table 6: Migrants by place of birth and age, INDIA 2001.

Age Group	Within the State		Outside the state in India		Born abroad	
	Persons	Percentage	Persons	Percentage	Persons	Percentage
All Ages	258641103	100.0	42341703	100.0	6168930	100.0
0-4	9060658	3.5	1343976	3.2	34365	0.6
5-9	11013578	4.3	1783998	4.2	54476	0.9
10-14	12924036	5.0	2029960	4.5	110046	1.8
15-24	45095896	17.4	7824658	18.5	434648	7.0
25-34	59875997	23.2	10458756	24.7	664932	10.8
35-59	91972022	35.6	15290835	38.1	2572225	41.7
60+	28151029	10.9	3538137	8.4	2285361	37.1
Age not Stated	547887	0.2	71383	0.2	10887	0.2

Source: Table D-1 Appendix, Census of India 2001.

Among male migrants in the country, 44.90% are in rural India and 55.10% in urban India, whereas the corresponding distribution for female migrants is 77.94% in rural India and 22.06% in urban India. However, around one-fifth of the urban growth is accounted for by rural to urban net migration. The gross decadal inflow of rural to urban migrants as a percentage of total urban population in 2001 turns out to be a little above 7 percent at the all-India level. However, it varies considerably across states. Both industrialized states like Gujarat and Maharashtra and the backward states like Orissa and Madhya Pradesh show high rates of migration. Similarly, examples can be found from both the types of states which have recorded sluggish migration rate, e.g., industrialized states such as Tamil Nadu and West Bengal and backward states like Uttar Pradesh, Bihar and Rajasthan. Hence, it is not possible at this stage to draw any clear-cut conclusion regarding the magnitude of the migration rate in relation to the nature of the states.

The present study addresses the question of the relationship between population change and migration with emphasis on the changes that occur in economic development. Migration is as old as man himself. It is one of the principal causes, along with natural increase or decrease of population, for fluctuations in population. Migration may be motivated by various causes, among which are personal, political, economic, and natural forces. Migration currents acquire significant prominence with technological advance and industrial development since redistribution of population is likely to occur with development. Since migration results in the redistribution of population, its study assumes great importance in the analysis of demographic data. The object of this study is to evaluate the place of birth criterion used by census, discuss the nature and consequences of internal movements of population, rather than migration at one point of time, and consider urban areas development as a measure to control migration

Table 7: Total Gross Decadal Migrants as a percent to Total Urban Population in 2001.

States	Rural to Urban Migrants (1991-2001) as a % of Urban Population
Andhra Pradesh	6.72
Assam	7.12
Bihar	6.28
Gujarat	10.63
Haryana	11.45
Karnataka	7.03
Kerala	6.99
Madhya Pradesh	9.50
Maharashtra	10.41
Orissa	10.97

Punjab	7.63
Rajasthan	6.18
Tamil Nadu	3.34
Uttar Pradesh	4.44
West Bengal	4.83
All India	7.32

Source: Census of India 2001, Migration Table.[2]

The sex wise differences are more prominent in Indian migration data. In 2001, 20.65 percent male and 40.95 percent female population were enumerated outside their place of birth in Karnataka. The prevailing marriage custom in India of groom after marriage terms most of female as migrants. It was noted that both Karnataka and Indian migration percentage has declined from 1871 to 2001. Whereas the percentage of non-migrant population has increased during the same period. The percentage of Karnataka migrants however in all these three censuses has been slightly higher than in India as a whole, the percentage of male migrants in Karnataka also is much higher than in India. However, it is striking to note that the percentage of female migrants is lower in Karnataka compared to India as a whole.

The internal migration data are presented in census reports at three levels viz., Inter-district, Intra-district, and Inter-state. Based on types of migration streams, data is presented in Table 8 for 2001. It includes that distance plays an important role in the migration process.

Table 8: Gross Decadal Intra and Inter State Migration of Males and Females as a percentage of Total Male and Females Urban Population in 2001.

2 Migration is defined as the gross decadal (1991-2001) inflow of inter and inter-state rural to urban migration (based on the last residence concept) as a percentage of total urban population (2001). Bihar includes Jharkhand, Madhya Pradesh includes Chhattisgarh and Uttar Pradesh includes Uttaranchal.

States	Intra State Male	**Intra State Female**	Inter State Male	Inter State Female	Intra+ Inter State Male	Intra+ Inter State Female
Andhra Pradesh	6.11	6.59	0.39	0.34	6.5	6.93
Arunachal Pradesh	13.39	14.82	7.67	7.17	21.06	21.99
Assam	5.75	6.22	1.25	0.93	7.01	7.15
Bihar	4.14	6.83	0.42	0.7	4.56	7.53
Chhattisgarh	6.58	8.64	2.22	2.38	8.8	11.02
Gujarat	6.78	8.33	3.89	2.21	10.67	10.54
Haryana	4.56	6.72	6.09	5.38	10.65	12.09
Himachal Pradesh	13.37	14.48	8.09	4.65	21.46	19.13
Jammu & Kashmir	3.03	3.29	1.46	1.48	4.49	4.77
Jharkhand	2.71	3.93	1.46	1.48	4.49	4.77
Karnataka	5.38	6.16	1.36	1.16	6.74	7.32
Kerala	4.81	8.06	0.6	0.4	5.41	8.46
Madhya Pradesh	5.09	6.95	1.26	1.56	6.35	8.51
Maharashtra	5.83	7.18	4.77	2.92	10.6	10.09
Meghalaya	2.26	2.51	2.08	1.47	4.34	3.98
Mizoram	7.08	7.7	2.28	1.15	9.36	8.85
Nagaland	4.11	3.91	3.34	2.53	7.45	6.44
Orissa	9.44	10.31	1.1	1.1	10.54	11.41
Punjab	2.58	4.76	4.8	2.88	7.38	7.64
Rajasthan	4.17	5.92	1.15	1.18	5.32	7.1
Sikkim	7.04	8.2	6.26	5.23	13.31	13.42
Tamil Nadu	2.78	3.44	0.22	0.22	2.99	3.66
Tripura	6.18	8.37	0.4	0.38	6.58	8.75
Uttar Pradesh	2.66	4.33	0.59	0.64	3.25	4.97
Uttaranchal	5.43	6.04	4.24	4.18	9.67	10.22
West Bengal	2.45	4.23	1.43	1.11	3.88	5.34
Andaman & Nicobar	4.43	4.89	8.81	6.75	13.24	11.65
Chandigarh	0.12	0.1	13.99	12.79	14.11	12.89
Dadar & Nagar Haveli	0.35	0.31	29.15	19.98	29.5	20.29

Daman & Diu	0.24	0.2	8.89	5.96	9.12	6.16
Delhi	0.09	0.14	11.25	9.43	11.34	9.57
Goa	4.4	6.67	6.7	5.46	11.1	12.13
Lakshadweep	11.16	9.56	3.38	0.61	14.54	10.17
Pondicherry	1.68	1.86	4.88	6.2	6.55	8.06

Source: Based on Population Census, 2001.

Marriage and employment are the major reasons for migration, Census data show. The bulk of the migration takes place within individual states — out of the total number of persons registered as "migrants" in the 2011 Census, only 11.91% (5.43 crore) had moved to one state from another, while nearly 39.57 crore had moved within their states. Migration data to and from some major states are given in the table above. Some key highlights of the Census numbers: Of the 5.74 crore migrants in Maharashtra, 27.55 lakh reported their last place of residence to be Uttar Pradesh; 5.68 lakh said Bihar. Internal migration from within Maharashtra had the lion's share of migrants: 4.79 crore. UP, from where people travel to all over India in search of work, itself was host to 5.65 crore migrants. As many as 5.20 crore were, however, internal migrants; among the 40.62 lakh from other Indian states, 10.73 lakh were from Bihar. The number of migrants in Punjab from other states was 24.88 lakh, a relatively large percentage of its total 1.37 crore migrant population. Of these, 6.50 lakh reported their previous residence to be in UP; 3.53 lakh said Bihar.

Over 42% of the 39.16 lakh 'outsiders' (from other states) in Gujarat (out of the total migrant population of 2.69 crore) were made up by migrants from UP (9.29 lakh) and Rajasthan (7.47 lakh), the data show.in Assam, where illegal migrations from Bangladesh has long been an issue, Census 2011 recorded 64,117 people who said their last place of residence was in the neighboring country. This was a little more than half of the total number of migrants (1,10,314) from outside India in the state. Among the 4.96 lakh migrants from other Indian states in Assam, those from Bihar had the largest stare (1.47 lakh, or nearly 30%).

Table 9: Percentage distribution of lifetime internal migration stream in India 1971-2001.

Type of migration	1971			1981			1991			2001		
	Male	Female	Total	Male	Female	Total	Male	Female	Total	Male	Female	Total
R-R	53.2	77.6	70.0	45.6	73.3	65.2	43.4	76.5	67.2	36.4	72.3	62.9
R -U	26.6	10.7	15.6	3.0	12.5	17/6	31.6	8.4	13.9	34.2	13.5	18.9
U -R	6.4	5.0	5.5	7.0	5.6	5.9	7.2	5.8	6.2	6.3	4.2	4.8
U-U	13.8	6.7	8.9	17.4	8.6	11.3	17/8	9.3	11.7	23.1	10.0	13.4
Total	100	100	100	100	100	100	100	100	100	100	100	100
Rural loss	20.2	5.7	10.1	23	6.9	11.7	24.4	26	7.7	27.9	9.3	14.1

Sources: (1) Census of India, 1971, series-1, Part-II-D(2), Migration Tables.

(2) Census Of India,1981, Series-I, Part V-A & b(i), Migration Tables.

The above Table-9 gives the distribution of life-time internal migration (based on birthplace data) for different migration streams occurred in to last four censuses, i.e., 1971 to 2001. A comparison of the 2001 Census migration data with 1991 Census shows high growth (32.9%) in the number of total migrants by place of birth, which is more than the natural growth of the population.

Table 10: Urbanization in India 1901-2001.

Census Year	% of Urban Population in total	Urban Population(million)	Difference over the previous decade	No of Towns
1901	10.85	25.6	-	1827
1911	10.29	25.9	0.1	1815
1921	11.18	28.1	2.2	1949
1931	11.99	33.5	5.4	2072
1941	13.86	44.1	10.6	2250
1951	17.29	62.4	18.3	2843
1961	17.97	76.9	16.5	2365
1971	19.91	109.1	30.2	2500
1981	23.34	159.4	50.3	3378
1991	25.71	217.6	58.2	3768
2001	27.78	285.4	67.8	-

Source: Census Reports.

Greater research as well as significant restructuring of the system of governance, legal and administrative framework is required in a manner that standard reform measures can be implemented. Urbanization refers to a change of residence (places) from traditional rural economies to modern industrial ones. It is a progressive concentration (Davis, 1965) of a Population in an urban unit. Quantification of urbanization is exceedingly difficult. It is a long-term process. Davis has explained urbanization as a process (Davis, 1962) of switch fromspread out pattern of human settlements to one of concentration in urban centers. It is a finite process- a cycle through which a nation passes as they evolve from agrarian to industrial society (Davis and Golden, 1954). Accordingly, three stages in the process of urbanization are mentioned. Stage one is the initial stage characterized by rural traditional society with predominance in agriculture and dispersed pattern of settlements. Stage two refers to an acceleration stage where basic restructuring of the economy and investments in social overhead capitals including transportation, communication (Pranati, 2006). Proportions of urban population gradually increase from 25% to 40%, 50%, 60% and soon. Dependence on primary sector gradually dwindles. The third stage is known as terminal stage where urban population exceeds 70% or more. At this stage level of urbanization (Davis, 1965) remains same or constant. Rate of growth of urban population and total population becomes same at this terminal stage.

A change in the usual place of residence can take place either permanent or semi-permanent or temporary basis or seasonal. However, there is no standard source of data either for internal or international migration (Bell, 2003; United Nations, 2002). Some social scientists have surveyed districts, areas and states and have also reported about migration scenarios. A recent survey shows that census is the largest source of information on internal migration at the cross-country level. A study shows that 138countries collected information on internal migration in their censuses compared to 35through registers and 22 from surveys (Bell, 2003). Migration can be measured in several ways with two most common forms of data being events and transitions. The former are normally associated with population registers, which record individual moves while the latter is generally derived from censuses comparing place of residence at two points in time. Population registers in fact count the migrations, while the census counts the migrants (Boden et al. 1992). In India, it is very complex to accurately identify migrants because they are not required to be registered in India either at their place of origin or their destination. This exacerbates problems including illegal settlements and other terrorist activities such as bomb explosions at public places. This contrasts with the practice in China where migrants are required to register themselves with the local authority (Zhu 2003). In lack of registration of migrants, Census and National Sample Survey Organization (NSSO)are the two main sources of migration data in India. Census provides data on migrants based on place of birth and place of last residence. If the place of birth or place of last residence is different from the place of enumeration, a person is defined as a migrant(Bhagat; 2005) On the other hand, if the place of birth and place of numeration is the same, the person is a non-migrant. Migrants defined based on place of birth or place of last residence are called lifetime migrants because the time of their move is unknown (Visaria 1980). It has also been observed that the migrants from rural areas retain attachment to their native place. They continue to maintain links with their families and villages through regular visits and sending remittances (Singh et al 1980). However, the lifetime migration based on census definition does not provide information on the number of moves made by a migrant.

Indian census provides information on place of birth for each person right from1881 census. The name of district was recorded if the person was born in the district other than the district of enumeration. Similarly, the name of the province was recorded if the person was born in the province other than province of enumeration. Until 1951census, the district was the lowest administrative unit of defining the place of birth. Based on this information it was possible to identify inter-district and inter-state migration but was not possible to identify intra-district migration. However, since 1961census, it was possible to measure intra-district migration as village or town was considered the unit of defining the place of birth (Srivastava 1972). It was possible for the first time to study the rural urban origin of migrants defined in relation to place of birth and four streams of migration viz. (i) rural to urban, (ii) urban to urban (iii) urban to rural and (iv) rural to rural (Bose 1976; Skeldon 1986). The duration of residence was also ascertained in 1961 census. Place of last residence was added in since 1971census and the reasons of migration related to place of last residence were also asked since 1981 census. Currently developed countries are characterized by high levels of urbanization and some of them are in the final stage of the urbanization process and subsequently are experiencing a slowing down of urbanization due to a host of factors (Brockerhoff,1999; Brockerhoff and Brennam 1998). Most of the developing countries, on the other hand, started experiencing urbanization only since the middle of the 20th century. The main objective of this study is to identify the process of urbanization in India with emphasis on level, ratio of urban and rural, rate of migration using the Indian Census data 1901-2001. It tries to trace the pattern of urbanization, urban problems and future projection of population of urban and cities and related policy issues as well.

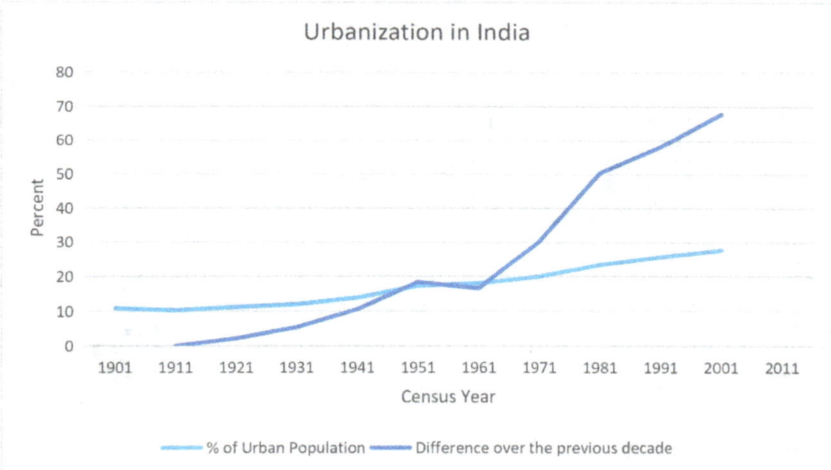

Trend and future estimation

Table 11, shows the trend and future estimation of urban-rural ratio to rural population. The trend of urbanization is calculated through time series analyses and urban-rural ratio (U/R*100) is used to measure urban ratio to rural ratio. From above table the percentage of the rural population gradually decreases from 89% to 72% over a century whereas, the percentage of the urban population has increased from 11% in1901 to 28 % in 2001. By the year 2051, it is projected that more than 36% of the total population will be residing in urban area, while urban-rural ratio may increase by more than 56% by 2051.Trend of Urbanization can be seen from the Graph. If, according to the projections, the Urban-rural ratio for India in 2051 will turn out to be 56, it means that against every 100 rural population there will be 56 urbanites in India. However, according to literature (Mathur 2004), the process of urbanization in India is likely to persist until2030 A.D. at least unless, it is estimated to achieve a level of 50 % urbanization.

Table 11: Trends in Urbanization

Census Year	% of urban to total population	Trend (% of urban pop to total)	% of rural population to total pop	Urban-Rural ratio(%)
1901	10.85	8.07	89.15	12.17
1911	10.29	9.92	89.71	11.47
1921	11.18	11.76	88.82	12.59
1931	11.99	13.60	88.01	13.62
1941	13.86	15.44	86.14	16.09
1951	17.29	17.29	82.71	20.90
1961	17.97	19.13	82.03	21.91
1971	19.91	20.97	80.09	24.86
1981	23.34	22.82	76.66	3045
1991	25.71	24.66	74.29	34.61
2001	27.78	26.50	72.22	38.47
2011		28.16		39.20
2021		30.19		43.25
2031		32.03		47.13
2041		33.88		51.23
2051		35.72		55.57

Source: Census of India.

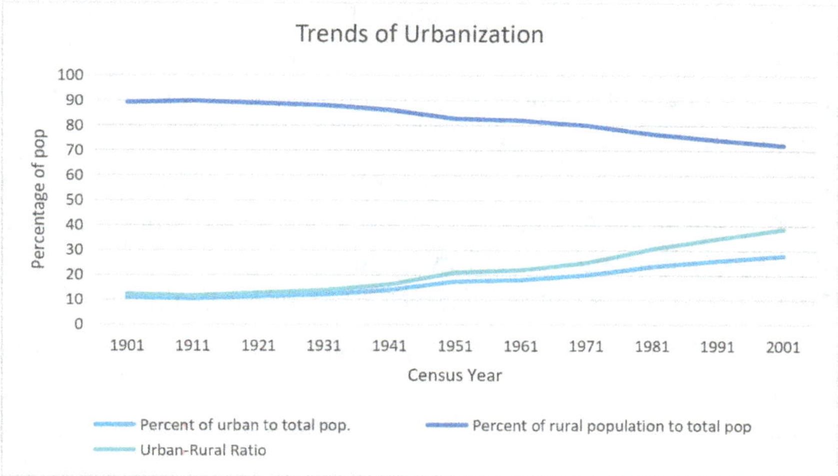

Stream and Volume of Internal migration

Data shows that stream and volume of internal migration by place of last residence1991 and 2001 in (duration 0-9). It is clear from the data that follows, that most of the female migrants migrating from rural to rural through marriage migration in intra state(68.6%) and interstate (32.7%) as well as international migration, While the total percentage of migrant rural to rural in inter state migrants (38%) is greater in comparison to rural to rural in intra-state migrants. Past studies have also reported that several migrants have been migrating within the district, within the state as well as within the nation. This is the reason for the larger number of migrants being categorized as intrastate migrants.

Urbanization is crucially linked to migration. Whether migration is a strong or a weak force in the urbanization process depends upon the nature and pattern of migration. Apart from economic reasons, migration occurs due to a host of socio-cultural and other factors. Before the contribution of migration in urban growth is discussed, it would be worthwhile to mention the nature and source of migration data in India.

Internal migration in India is many times larger than international migration. The critical issue is how to reduce the impact of push factors and augment the impact of pull factors so that return on investment in human capital could be maximized? Many have argued that it would be inappropriate to prevent migration as it plays a very important role in development and in fulfilling human aspirations. Preventing migration could even be counterproductive (UNDP 2009; World Bank 2009; UNESCO 2013; Foresight 2011). The recent UNESCO (2013) publication highlighted that the policies and programs facilitating integration of migrants at the destination remain weak at best or non-existent and suggested the inclusion and integration of migrants in development. However, it is necessary to emphasize that migration is very intrinsic to the path of human development, but its impact is also place specific (de Haan 2011). Policies that lower the costs of migration, eliminate discrimination against migrants, and protect their rights can reap even bigger gains for development (Sutherland 2013). A continued understanding of urban transition is also essential for developing an appropriate spatial strategy of urbanization which is just and sustainable. In the context of India, there is a need to integrate migration in urbanization and development policies.

Table 12: Gross Decadal Intra and Inter State Migration of Male and Female as a Percent of Total Male and Female Urban Population in 2001.

States	Intra state	Intra state	Inter State	Inter State	Inter+Intra	Inter+Intra
	Male	Female	Male	Female	Male	Female
Andhra Pradesh	6.11	6.59	0.39	0.34	6.5	6.93
Arunachal Pradesh	13.39	14.82	7.67	7.17	21.06	21.99

Assam	5.75	6.22	1.25	0.93	7.01	7.15
Bihar	4.14	6.83	0.42	0.7	4.56	7.53
Chhattisgarh	6.58	8.64	2.22	2.38	8.8	11.02
Gujrat	6.78	8.33	3.89	2.21	10.67	10.54
Haryana	4.56	6.72	6.09	5.38	10.65	12.09
Himachal Pradesh	13.37	14.48	8.09	4.65	21.46	19.13
Jammu & Kashmir	3.03	3.29	1.46	1.48	4.49	4.77
Jharkhand	2.71	3.93	3.02	3.8	5.73	7.73
Karnataka	5.38	6.16	1.36	1.48	4.49	4.77
Kerala	4.81	8.06	0.6	0.4	5.41	8.46
Madhya Pradesh	5.09	6.95	1.26	1.56	6.35	8.51
Maharashtra	5.83	7.18	4.77	2.92	10.6	10.09
Meghalaya	2.28	2.51	2.08	1.47	4.34	3.98
Mizoram	7.08	7.7	2.28	1.15	9.36	8.85
Nagaland	4.11	3.91	3.34	2.53	7.45	6.44
Orissa	9.44	10.31	1.1	1.1	10.54	11.41
Punjab	2.58	4.76	4.8	2.88	7.38	7.64
Rajasthan	4.17	5.92	1.15	1.18	5.32	7.1
Sikkim	7.04	8.2	6.26	5.23	13.31	13.42
Tamil Nadu	2.78	3.44	0.22	0.22	2.99	3.66
Tripura	6.18	8.37	0.4	0.38	6.58	8.75
Uttar Pradesh	2.66	4.33	0.59	0.64	3.25	4.97
Uttaranchal	5.43	6.04	4.24	4.18	9.67	10.22
West Bengal	2.45	4.23	1.43	1.11	3.88	5.34
Andaman & Nicobar	4.43	4.89	8.81	6.75	13.34	11.65
Chandigarh	0.12	0.1	13.99	12.79	14.11	12.89

Dadar & Nagar Haveli	0.35	0.31	29.15	19.98	29.5	20.29
Daman & Diu	0.24	0.2	8.89	5.96	9.12	6.16
Delhi	0.09	0.14	11.25	9.43	11.34	9.57
Goa	4.4	6.67	6.7	5.46	11.1	12.13
Lakshadweep	11.16	9.56	3.38	0.61	14.54	10.17
Pondicherry	1.68	1.86	4.88	6.2	6.55	8.06

Source: Census Of India, 2001.

Reasons for migration

Data shows the reasons for migration, and the percentage of migrants at their last residence with duration (0-9 years). Most of male migrants (37.6%) cited Work/Employment as the main reason. 43.8% migrants, who cited 'Marriage' follows this, and finally, 'Moved with households' was cited as the third highest indicator. The rationale behind this is that a greater number of educated, skilled and unskilled people move to other states for better opportunities, to earn larger incomes, and in search of a job respectively. The percentages of male and female migrants that

'Moved with households' were found to be second highest 25.1% and 19% respectively. It may be

because most migrants want to move with their families from their native places. In the year 2001 the migration scenario changed. While past studies (Singh and Yadav, 1991) reported that higher single male migrants in comparison to those who 'Moved with households', they maintained a connection to their place of origin by sending remittances. A study reveals that more educated, skilled, and larger income holders are likely to migrate (2001 census report).

Migrants and their educational level

The data shows the percentage distribution of migrants and their educational level. The data indicates that the percentages of all educational levels, beside illiterate females, were found to be approximately the same for both migrants and non- migrant households. The percentage of females were found to be higher for migrant households in comparison to non-migrant households, While the percentage of males in non-migrant households is approximately two times (17.3%) that of the males in migrant households. This may be due to fact that illiterate migrants were not required at destination places because skilled persons or comparatively educated persons are only required at destination places. Whereas female migrants have been working in houses doing domestic chores, the other reason reflected in the study, was migration due to marriage.

Worthwhile to note that urban population growth alone cannot speed up urbanization. More importantly, if urbanization must occur, the urban population growth rate needs to be higher than the rural population growth rate. Thus, it is the urban-rural population growth differential that is critical to the process of urbanization. The data shows that urban-rural growth differentials increased from about 1% per annum during 1991-2001 to 1.61% per annum during 2001-2011. It is also evident from the data that the rural population growth has declined much faster during 2001-2011 compared to earlier decades. Note that the urban-rural population growth differential is a product of the differentials in the natural increase between rural and urban areas (births-deaths), net rural urban classification and net rural-to-urban migration. The urban-rural natural increase growth differentials remained almost constant (4 per 1,000 population) during 1991-2000 to 2001-2010. Therefore, it was the net rural-urban classification and net rural-to-urban migration that were responsible for higher urban-rural growth differentials and the speeding up of urbanization during 2001-2011.

Components of Urban Growth

The natural increase, net rural-urban classification and rural-to-urban migration are components of urban population growth. An assessment of their relative contributions is very important to understand the dynamics of urban population growth. The contribution of net rural-urban classification and rural-to-urban migration has increased from 42% in 1991-2001 to 56% in 2001-2011. The available data from the 2011 Census now does not allow for the separation of these two factors, but it does show the emergence of a large number of new towns in 2011. The number of towns at the national level increased from 5,161 to 7,935 – a net addition of 2,774 towns (2,532 census towns and 242 statutory towns) in 2011 compared to the 2001 Census.

As there has been no change in the definition of the urban between the 2001 and 2011 censuses, this has contributed significantly to faster urbanization despite several metropolitan cities showing a huge decline in their growth rates (Kundu 2011). On the other hand, the contribution of natural increases in urban population growth has declined from a peak of 62% during 1981-91 to 44% during 2001-2011. Yet the natural increase added a huge population of about 40 million in the urban areas during 2001-2011. In the study of India's urbanization, the contribution of natural increases has not received as much attention as rural-to-urban migration. This has led to the popular belief that the urban population is increasing solely due to migration.

Variation in migration profile (1991-2001)

The data indicates the variation in migration profile between the years 1991 and 2001 for some important states based on migrants by last residence (0-9years). The rate of outmigration was found to be high (3.4) for Bihar, and it is followed closely by Delhi (3.3).

The reason is that Bihar's migrants have marginal land or no land to sustain a livelihood, and Delhi's migrants are economically strong and they wanted to migrate for a better opportunity to earn a larger income. Shukla (2002) has reported earlier in the study of U.P. state that two types of migration trends were found to be more prevalent, those who have marginal land or no land and others who are economically strong. In the case of Bihar, the rate of migration was exceedingly high (3.4%) in the 2001 census whereas it was found to be 1.9% in 1991 census. Growth rate of the net migration in 2001 was found to be very high (34.3%) for Haryana. From the data, the percentage growth rate of in-migration was found to be substantially higher (76%) in comparison to outmigration (4.7%). This is an eye-opening concern to the government body and the policy makers. Punjab, Haryana, and Maharashtra, which are on top of the list in (SDP) State domestic product per capita and where the poverty percentage is low, attract migrants from other states. Whereas Bihar, which has high population growth rate, high levels of poverty and poor SDP, has out migration exceeding in-migration by 31 for every 1000 persons.

States-wise change in growth and migration

The data shows that state-wise change in growth and migration. From the data it is evident that Punjab, Haryana, and Maharashtra, which top the list in SDP per-capita and where the poverty percentage is low, attract migrants from other states. Whereas the international migration of labor is an important component of globalization and economic development in many less developed countries. The number of international migrants, or people residing in a country other than their country of birth, has increased more, or less linearly over the past 40 years. Recent economic studies suggest that migration and development are closely linked to one another. Development shapes migration, and migration, in turn, influences development. India has seen an upsurge in economic growth since 1991. The 2001 census shows that internal migration has picked up rapidly during the 1900's. Compared to intra-state (short distance) movement, inter-state (long distance) migration has grown faster. The state with higher per capita income and larger dominance of non-agricultural sector shows not only high in-migration but also high out-migration rates. Poverty ratio is not found related with out-migration rates at the state level. On the contrary, migration rates are higher in households with higher monthly per capita expenditure. Also, the socially disadvantaged groups like Scheduled Caste and Scheduled Tribes do not show higher mobility compared to other population categories. Thus, the increased mobility of India's population in recent times is more confined to better off section.

India has embarked upon the new economic policy in the year 1991 popularly known as liberalization of the Indian economy. Migration is one of the three basic components of population growth of any region (other two are fertility and mortality). It plays a significant role in improving economic and social conditions of people. Few factors play an important role in decision to move, like economic, social, cultural and political factors. Migration affects not only the size but also the composition of the population of both origin and destination. Migration has a special significance for the developing countries.

It has been accepted that the cause-effect relationship between population change, and migration can go in either direction. That is, population change once generated has considerable influence on the migration and vice-versa. That they are mutually inter-dependent and interacting hardly needs to be emphasized. There is need to understand the nature of these changes, and there is even greater need to un revel the casual interrelations, if any. Consider an area with initially high mortality and fertility, where there has been a substantial decline in mortality,

1) Assume that this decline in mortality has been due to some non-economic factors

2) With unchanging fertility (and migration), this results in an increase in the rate of natural increase and the rate of growth of population.

This increase in population may have far reaching implications on the consumption side, and after a lag of 15-20 years, when these enlarged cohorts begin to enter the productivity ages, on employment aspects as well. These new entrants to the labor force might also generate additional consumption requirements because they would be simultaneously entering their family forming age. This might necessitate changes in various aspects of agricultural development, and migration. They could be subsumed under the following headings:

1.Changes in the extent and pattern of land utilization,

2. Changes in inputs that might influence land and labor productivity,

3.Adoption and innovation of new agricultural technology, and Changes in agricultural organizations such as size of holdings, land tenure, etc. To the extent that these changes bring about changes in total and per capita output, mortality, migration, and fertility might be expected to change. Instead, if the initial development took place on the agricultural side, it might alter the course of mortality, fertility, and migration, and as a result, rate of growth of population would be affected. However, there is a growing controversy regarding the magnitude and direction of the influence of one upon the other, and this is more so regarding the influence of population change on migration. Migration according to census of India can also be classified into four different types based on administrative boundaries of a district and state. Intra-district migrants (short distance migration): If the person enumerated at different place but born within the district.

Inter-district migrants (medium distance migration): Persons born outside the district of enumeration but within the same state. In other words, inter-district migration relates to those migrants who move from one district to another district of the state.

Inter-state migrants (long distance migration): Persons enumerated in a state but born in the other state. International migrants: Persons enumerated in India born in other countries. The focus of this study is to analyze the trend and pattern of various types of migration, such as Intra-district, Inter-district, Inter-state, rural-rural, rural-urban. Urban-urban, and urban-rural migration in Karnataka and All India level and to analyze the reasons behind the migration. and All India level and to analyze the reasons behind the migration.

URBANIZING INDIA: THE 2011 CENSUS SHOWS SLOWING GROWTH

Provisional results from the 2011 census of India show a diminishing population, the lowest since independence in 1947. From 2001 to 2007, India's population grew 17.6%, compared to a 20% to 25% growth rate in previous periods since the 1951 census. Even so, India is expected to virtually catch up with China in population by 2020, with United Nations forecasts showing a less than 1 million advantage for China. By 2025, the UN forecasts that India will lead China by more than 50 million people. Nonetheless, like many other developing nations, falling birth rates are substantially reducing population growth in India.

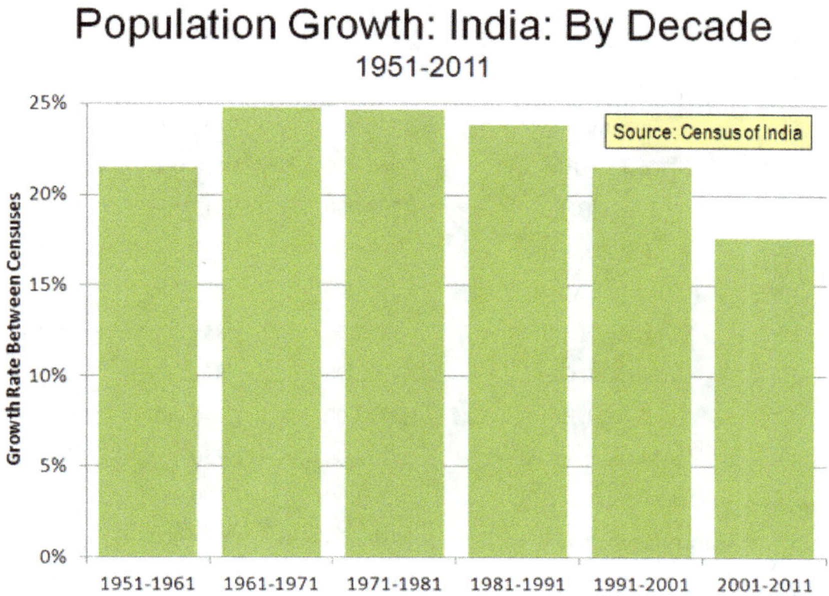

Table 13:Urban Areas Over 1,000,000 Population: 2011

Rank	Urban Area	2001	2011	% Change
1	Delhi, NCT-UP-HAR	15,358,000	21,622,000	41%
2	Mumbai, MAH	16,554,000	18,790,000	14%
3	Kolkata, WB	13,217,000	14,113,000	7%
4	Chennai, TN	6,425,000	8,696,000	35%
5	Bangalore, KAR	5,687,000	8,499,000	49%
6	Hyderabad, AP	5,534,000	7,749,000	40%
7	Ahmadabad, GUJ	4,519,000	6,352,000	41%
8	Pune, MAH	3,756,000	5,050,000	34%
9	Surat, GUJ	2,811,000	4,585,000	63%
10	Jaipur, RAJ	2,324,000	3,073,000	32%
11	Kanpur, UP	2,690,000	2,920,000	9%
12	Lucknow, UP	2,267,000	2,901,000	28%

13	Nagpur, MAH	2,123,000	2,498,000	18%
14	Indore, MP	1,639,000	2,167,000	32%
15	Coimbatore, TN	1,446,000	2,151,000	49%
16	Kochi, KER	1,355,000	2,118,000	56%
17	Patna, BH	1,707,000	2,047,000	20%
18	Kozhikode, KER	880,000	2,031,000	131%
19	Bhopal, MP	1,455,000	1,883,000	29%
20	Thrissur, KER	330,000	1,855,000	462%
21	Vadodara, GUJ	1,492,000	1,817,000	22%
22	Agra, UP	1,321,000	1,746,000	32%
23	Visakhapatnam, AP	1,329,000	1,730,000	30%
24	Malappuram, KER	170,000	1,699,000	899%
25	Thiruvananthapuram, KER	889,000	1,687,000	90%
26	Kannur, KER	498,000	1,643,000	230%
27	Ludhiana, PJ	1,395,000	1,614,000	16%
28	Nashik, MAH	1,152,000	1,563,000	36%
29	Vijayawada , AP	1,011,000	1,491,000	47%
30	Madurai, TN	1,195,000	1,462,000	22%
31	Varanasi, UP	1,212,000	1,435,000	18%
32	Meerut, UP	1,167,000	1,425,000	22%
33	Rajkot, GUJ	1,002,000	1,391,000	39%
34	Jamshedpur, JH	1,102,000	1,337,000	21%
35	Srinagar, JK	971,000	1,273,000	31%
36	Jabalpur, MP	1,117,000	1,268,000	14%
37	Asansol, WB	1,090,000	1,243,000	14%
38	Vasai Virar, MAH	293,000	1,221,000	317%
39	Allahabad, UP	1,050,000	1,217,000	16%
40	Dhanbad. JH	1,064,000	1,195,000	12%
41	Aurangabad, MAH	892,000	1,189,000	33%
42	Amritsar, PJ	1,011,000	1,184,000	17%
43	Jodhpur, RAJ	856,000	1,138,000	33%
44	Ranchi, JH	863,000	1,127,000	31%

45	Raipur , CHH	699,000	1,123,000	61%
46	Kollam, KER	380,000	1,110,000	192%
47	Gwalior, MP	866,000	1,102,000	27%
48	Durg-Bhilainagar, CHH	924,000	1,064,000	15%
49	Chandigarh, CH	809,000	1,026,000	27%
50	Tiruchirappalli, TN	847,000	1,022,000	21%
51	Kota, RAJ	705,000	1,001,000	42%

Data derived from Census of India

Delhi: Delhi (National Capital Territory, Uttar Pradesh, and Haryana) was reported by the United Nations to have become the second largest urban area in the world, following Tokyo in 2010. However, the Delhi urban area was nearly 1,000,000 people short of the population than projected by the United Nations. However, over the decade, Delhi managed to become the nation's largest urban area with a population of 21.6 million people, an increase of 41% over its 15.5 million people in 2001 (Note 1). This is an impressive accomplishment, since some demographers have long maintained that Mumbai could be destined to become the largest urban area in the world in future decades.

Mumbai: Mumbai (formerly Bombay), in Maharashtra, placed second with a population of 18.8 million. This compares to a population of 16.6 million in 2001. The Mumbai urban area grow only 14% between 2001 and 2011, a much slower rate than before, driven by declines in the urban core of central Mumbai – another general global phenomenon – and only modest growth in the suburban Mumbai portion of the central city, with explosive growth in the suburban areas outside the central city (Note 2). Mumbai's 2011 population is approximately 1.5 million below the level that would have been indicated by the 2010 United Nations projection

Chapter II

OBJECTIVE OF THE STUDY:

The objectives of this study are twofold: first, it aims to describe and compare the patterns of population change and magnitude of migration of an area and second, it tries to clarify the nature of casual inter-relation between the changes in population and migration factors. Karnataka is one of the major states of South India. With a total population over 66 million, Karnataka is the ninth largest states in India in terms of Population. Going by estimated figures of 2016, there are 66,076,021 people living in the state of Karnataka. The state enjoys a healthy lifestyle and is considered as one of the developed states of India. The population of the state was estimated to be 61,130,704 in 2011 Census of India. From there on, Karnataka has added another 4.9 million people to its growing population between years 2011 to 2016. Bangalore is the largest city in the state with over 1 million people living there. The state adds around 1 million people every year to its existing population. There are over 30 districts in the state of Karnataka. Among all the districts in the state, Bangalore Urban, Belgaum and Gulbarga are the most populated districts with a total head count of 3 million people in each district. Male to female ratio or Sex Ratio is quite good in the state with 964 females available for every 1000 males. In the last 30 years, Karnataka has been showing major signs of decline in its population growth. The state has witnessed a growth of 15.7 per cent in its population between years 2001 to 2011.

The southern state of Karnataka is currently home to over 66,076,021 (6.6 Crores) people. Every year, Karnataka adds around 1 million people to its growing population. In 2016, Population of Karnataka is estimated to be over 66 million. Population growth in Karnataka is considered to be satisfactory as compared with other populated states of India. Rapid industrialization and growth of various metros in Karnataka has contributed a lot towards its Population growth. Bangalore, the capital city witnessed a large number of migratory populations from other parts of India. So, with recent modernization in the state, Karnataka has witnessed a decent growth in its Population.

Migration was found to be substantially higher (76%) in comparison to out migration (4.7%). This is an eye-opening concern to the government body and the

policy makers. Punjab, Haryana and Maharashtra, which are on top of the list in (SDP) State domestic product per capita and where the poverty percentage is low, attract migrants from other

states. Whereas Bihar which has high population growth rate, high levels of poverty and poor SDP, has a migration exceeding in-migration by 31 for every 1000 persons. State-wise change in growth and migration. Table shows that states-wise change in growth and migration. From the table it is evident that Punjab, Haryana, and Maharashtra top the list in SDP per capita and where the poverty percentage is low, attract migrants from other states, whereas

Bihar which has high population growth rate has high levels of poverty and poor (SDP) State domestic product. West Bengal is another state, which receives more migrants from other states. The reason behind this is that there are number of migrants from Bangladesh as Bangladesh sharanarthi (refugee). In the case of Gujarat, the rate of in-migration is also high. This may be due to its industrial area, which draws people to move from other states. Maharashtra and Haryana have received a greater number of migrants in comparison to other states. In the case of Haryana, net-migration was found to be very high (79 per 1000 population), approximately twice that of Maharashtra. Haryana state has been attracting migrations from other districts, states as well as other countries. This may be due to the fact that this area is comparatively a highly developed area with a number of industries, shopping malls, call centers and so forth. There are different districts which are responsible for these, namely: Gurgaon, Faridabad, Rewari, Hishar, Panipat, and Sonipat. The Gurgaon district, especially have been attracting a large number of people from other areas because of a good environment, the standard of living, as well as a greater availability of jobs for skilled, semi-skilled and unskilled workers. Another reason attributed to high in-migrations from nearby states may be the close proximity to Delhi, the capital of India. The table below indicates the states of origin of the people drawn to Haryana.

Table 14: Current Population of Karnataka

Districts/state	Population in 2011			Growth Rate 2001-2011	Density (per Sq. Km)	Sex Ratio
	Persons	Male	Female	2001-11	2011	2011
Karnataka	61130704	31057742	30072962	15.67	319	968
Belgaum	4778439	2427104	2351335	13.38	358	969
Bagalkot	1890826	952902	937924	14.46	288	984
Bijapur	2175102	1112953	1062149	20.38	207	954
Bidar	1700018	870850	829168	13.16	312	952
Raichur	1924773	966493	958280	15.27	228	992
Koppal	1391292	701479	689813	16.32	250	983
Gadag	1065235	538477	526758	9.61	229	978
Dharwad	1846993	939127	907866	15.13	434	967
Uttar Kannada	1436847	727424	709423	6.15	140	975
Haveri	158506	819295	779211	11.08	331	951
Bellary	2532383	1280402	1251981	24.92	300	978
Chitradurga	1660378	843411	816967	9.39	197	969
Davanagere	1946905	989602	957303	8.71	329	967
Shimoga	1755512	879817	875695	6.88	207	995
Udupi	1177908	562896	615012	5.90	304	1093
Chikmagalur	1137753	567483	570270	-0.28	158	1005
Tumkur	2681449	1354770	1326679	3.74	253	979

Bangalore	9588910	5025498	4563412	46.68	4378	908
Mandya	1808680	909441	899239	2.55	365	989
Hassan	1776221	885807	890414	3.17	261	1005
Dakshina Kannada	2083625	1032577	1051048	9.80	457	1018
Kodagu	554762	274725	280037	1.13	135	1019
Mysore	2994744	1511206	1483538	13.39	437	982
Chamarajanagar	1020962	513359	507603	5.75	200	989
Gulbarga	2564892	1307061	1257831	17.94	233	962
Yadgir	1172985	591104	581881	22.67	224	984
Kolar	1540231	779041	760830	11.04	384	976
Chickballapur	1254377	637504	616873	9.17	298	968
Bangalore rural	987257	507514	479743	16.02	441	945
Ramanagara	1082739	548060	534679	5.06	303	976

The recorded experience of most of today's developed countries provide the necessary data for the analysis of the inter-relation between population change and migration, during the periods of their economic and demographic transition. Moreover, the developing countries are undergoing rapid declines in mortality, with little or no change in their level of fertility. There is also said to be occurring significant changes in agriculture. The ongoing experience of these countries also provides valuable information regarding the nature of these changes, and their inter-relations under different economic, demographic, social and cultural environment. It has tried to develop a framework within which one can analyze and compare the patterns of population change, and their components, and it has tried to provide some tentative answers to the questions of casual inter-relations between population change on the one hand and migration on the other in the context of the experience of Karnataka state and Its districts during the period 1951-2011. This is in addition to the information that is provided on the pattern of population change and their components.

The present study, however, has some disadvantages. Non-availability and unreliability of data have forced me to make "surmises" rather than "generalizations". At times I had to resort to very crude methods to estimate certain parameters. Even if adequate and reliable data were at hand it is difficult to make solid generalizations on the complex relationship between population change and migration and how much more difficult it would be if the data are inadequate and unreliable. If data on migration streams, and the changes therein were available then it would have been difficult to un reveal the forces behind these changes.

Given the above limitations, I would be happy if I am able to present a satisfactory framework for the analysis of population and migration, present some hypothesis regarding the casual inter-relations between population change and migration, and give some rather crude indications of differences among districts about population change, migration, and their components. It is necessary to consider the nature of movements of individuals rather than migration at one point of time. Often all types of movements are included under migration without any distinction, and this is misleading. First, there are seasonal movements of landless laborers and small peasants moving out of their villages to other villages and towns during the agricultural off-season looking for alternative jobs. They come back to their villages during the agricultural season. While some of them move out to find work wherever it exists, others move to the same place season after season to work with the same employer. This type of movement, although individual in character, is trans-humane. Trans-humane occurs as an organized effort in the case of certain trading castes. For instance, in Bhotias living on the border of Nepal have two sets of villages—one on the hill tops in which they live in summer and another on the plains for winter. This cycle of movement also facilitates their trade.

Secondly, there are itinerant traders and craftsmen such as the Banjara, the Gaddi Lohars and the Kallu Waddars who move from place to place on set routes, selling country cosmetics, household, and agricultural implements, and cutting stone and making grinding stones respectively. Itinerant movement is different from either trans-humane or seasonal movements; it involves several movements on longer routes and blurs the specificity of their places of origin.

Thirdly, there is a category of 'involuntary' movements which includes several variations. In marriage migration married women move from their natal villages or towns to their husband's villages and towns. In some cases (e.g., matrilineal Khasis) husbands move to wife's villages or towns. Child migration is also involuntary as children move with their parents. Government servants and others move from one place to another on transfer. Still another variation of involuntary migration occurs under extraordinary circumstances such as partition of nations, riots and floods. This may be called crisis migration. There is also displacement of persons due to a deliberate policy of the government to acquire villages for industrial purposes. Location of huge industrial plants has meant total uprooting of villages, causing out migration.

Fourthly, there is another kind of movement where people are recruited to work in plantations or in factories or in construction work through middlemen. Although indentured labor has stopped now, other forms of recruitment through agents do exist. Construction workers, for instance, move wherever the contractor moves.

Fifthly, there is the movement of commuters who are residents of villages on the fringe of cities and occasionally they may stay in their places of work for a few days. Commuting may be considered disguised migration because in the absence of their nearby village homes, they would have presumably migrated to their place of work.

Movement is neither unidirectional nor permanent. There is always movement back and forth, i.e., an adult does not move from village to the city always in steps (village-town-city), neither does he stay in the city for the rest of his life. The presence of relatives, vagaries of unemployment and retirement are some of the forces which encourage further shifts, returns and oscillations.

However, the major type of movement of people has been from rural areas to urban and especially metropolitan centers in search of employment which involves different phases and processes. Migration is brought about by many interacting factors, and it is unwise to build mono-casual explanations in terms of distances, or the availability of opportunities at the place of destination, or the conditions of distress at the place of origin. Whether a city is near or distant, is not important. Often people migrate to distant cities because they have a relative or a friend who is willing to help. Thus, a city which is physically distant, is socially near, and vice-versa. Similarly, it is not always true that only the poor would migrate. It is necessary to study the decision making process in the contexts of family organization, the stage of development of the family, dispersed kinship and friendship networks, sources and flows of information, the image of the prospective migrants about different cities, physical distance, economic situations, availability of alternative opportunities, skill potential and personality of migrants, In order to understand why people migrate, it would be necessary to enquire into the question why they do not, and under what conditions migration becomes stable or unstable.

Hear attempt has been done to analyze the trend and pattern of various types of migration, such as Intra-district, Inter-district, Inter-state, rural-rural, rural-urban, urban-urban, and urban-rural migration in Karnataka and India and try to analyze the reason behind the migration.

Table 15: Distribution of population in percentage by migration status in Karnataka and India 1971-2001. (Birthplace criterion)

Year	1971			1981			1991			2001		
	Total %	Male %	Female %	Total %	Male %	Female %	Total %	Male %	Female %	Total %	Male %	Female %
Karnataka (Pop in Million)												
Mig	31.3	23.2	39.7	31.5	22.4	41.0	29.6	20.0	39.5	30.6	20.7	41.0
N M	68.7	76.8	60.3	68.5	77.4	59.0	70.4	80.0	60.5	69.4	79.4	59.1
Pop	29.3	15.0	14.3	37.1	18.9	18.2	45.0	23.0	22.0	53.0	26.9	26.0
India (Pop in Million)												
Mig	30.4	18.9	42.8	30.6	17.8	44.3	27.4	14.6	41.2	29.9	17.0	44.0
N M	69.6	81.1	57.2	81.0	57.2	55.7	72.6	85.4	58.8	70.1	83.0	56.5
Pop	548	284	264	665	344	321	839	435	403	1028	532	496

Source: Migration tables of Karnataka and India from 1971 2001 census.

From Table 15, we know that the migration statistics which indicates that people of both Karnataka and India are becoming less mobile in nature. In the 2001 census, 16.2 million persons out of total population of 52.8 million in Karnataka were enumerated at a place different from the place of birth and thus termed as migrants. This constitutes 30.62 percent of the total population of the state. In terms of absolute figures, number has increased from 9.1 million in 1971 to 11.7 million in 1981 to 13.3 million in 1991 and 16.2 million in 2001. It may, however, be noted that the percentage of migrants to total population has constantly declined from 31.26 percent in 1971 to 30.62 percent in 2001. In terms of total volume of migration in India has increased from 166.8 million in 1971, 203.5 million in 1981, 229.8 million in 1991 and 307.1 million in 2001. The percentage of migrants to total population of the country has also decreased from 30.42 percent in 1971 to 29.86 percent in 2001.

In some parts of India, three out of four households include a migrant.

Table 16: Migrants in each Category according to reason for migration – all migrants 1991

	Reason For Migration							
	Employment		Education		Marriage		Others	
	Male	Female	Male	Female	Male	Female	Male	Female
Total Migrants	26.9	1.80	4.84	0.82	3.99	76.12	29.6	9.45
Within India	27.79	1.79	5.02	0.82	4.13	76.97	28.39	8.95
Within States	24.02	1.60	5.39	0.79	4.72	78.93	31.47	8.94
Intra district	18.08	1.21	5.44	0.70	5.69	81.04	37.07	9.03
Other District	33.96	2.65	5.31	1.04	3.11	72.10	22.10	8.68
Other States	43.42	3.76	3.48	1.11	1.67	60.14	15.65	9.06
Outmigrants From								
Andhra Pradesh	37.67	3.74	5.80	1.45	2.22	56.58	19.06	11.59
Assam	28.97	3.87	3.61	1.41	2.18	42.95	21.83	12.18
Bihar	51.21	4.52	3.67	0.98	1.77	62.76	13.62	7.45
Gujarat	27.68	2.28	4.90	1.43	1.59	56.39	22.17	14.60
Haryana	38.64	1.64	3.15	0.66	1.76	73.05	13.01	5.41
Himachal Pradesh	48.70	3.58	4.50	1.56	1.94	58.27	14.01	8.07
Karnataka	33.55	3.69	3.38	1.12	1.81	57.81	24.86	14.72
Kerala	52.65	10.85	4.04	3.33	1.44	41.42	15.25	14.04
Madya Pradesh	31.68	2.72	3.16	0.66	2.80	72.12	22.98	7.94
Maharashtra	34.32	4.60	2.47	0.90	1.95	55.92	24.00	12.63
Orissa	54.61	5.21	3.20	0.89	2.06	64.77	13.44	7.61
Punjab	32.48	2.47	2.39	1.08	1.09	57.38	15.59	7.45
Rajasthan	36.82	2.66	2.58	0.68	1.56	68.36	15.07	7.64
Tamil Nadu	47.76	8.27	2.68	1.14	2.71	46.59	15.06	11.67
Uttar Pradesh	53.07	3.13	3.12	1.03	0.96	57.27	9.80	6.62
West Bengal	40.72	2.89	3.89	1.06	2.00	68.75	15.96	6.22

Source: Migration Tables, 1991 Census, D-3.

India is on the pick of its demographic dividends as per the recent Census 2011. On an average 61 percent people are in working age (15-59). But the work participation rate is substantially low (39.8 per cent or 0.48 billion) that was slightly improved from previous census, 2001 (39.1 per cent). There is also wide variation for the states in work force participation rate from 51.9 per cent for Himachal Pradesh to 32.9 per cent for Uttar Pradesh. Lack of job opportunities associated with regional disparities, poverty, regional imbalance in the development, different developmental policies adopted by states, caste, class, and gender discrimination and somewhat inadequate reporting especially for female are the main reason for low work participation in India. Within the workforce participation, a substantial proportion of workers are in the marginal category (24.8 percent) i.e., person who work for less than six months and its share has also increased by 2.5 per cent point from 2001. Meanwhile, main workers who work for more than six months have declined at the same rate. Regional variation in workforce, economic opportunities and growing marginal workers lead to huge mobility from one part of India to another part. Towards urban or urban centric migration from rural rather than urban to urban is the unique pattern of Indian migration. Urban centric economic growth or policies promotes economic growth around preexisting growth centers in the advance regions (Kundu,2011a; Kundu an Sasikumar, 2005) is the responsibility for that. With the sluggish urbanization, the rate of migration in India has been declining during the last decade (Kundu, 2011a; Kundu and Saraswati,2012). Due to exclusionary urbanization, urban peripheries undergone through 'elite capture' and changed the economic pattern that reduces the absorption capacity of the cities for rural migrants (Kundu, 2011b, Kundu and Saraswathi, 2012). However, internal mobility balances the demand and supply of labor and helps to flourish the economy at the place of destination as well as reduce the poverty at the place of origin through remittance flow (Srivastav, 2011a, 2011b).

The sex wise difference is more prominent in Indian migration data. In 2001, 20.65 per cent male and 40.95 per cent female population was enumerated outside their place of birth in Karnataka. The prevailing marriage custom in India of brides moving to place of groom after marriage terns most of females as migrants. As seen above at both Karnataka and Indian migration percentage has declined from 1971 to 2001. Whereas the percentage of non-migrant population has increased during the same period. The percentage of Karnataka migrants however in all these three censuses has been slightly higher than in India as a whole, the percentage of male migrants in Karnataka also is much higher than in India. However, it is striking to note that the percentage of female migrants is lower in Karnataka compared to India as a whole.

Table 17: Net Migration Ratios in India

State	Net Migration Rate 1991-2001	Net Migration Rate 2007-08	Estimated Net Migration Rate 2001-11
Andhra Pradesh	-0.3	-0.87	-2.02
Assam	-0.7	-0.5	-2.21
Bihar	-2.7	-5.64	-3.39
Gujarat	1.7	1.63	1.64
Haryana	4.1	3.52	2.01
Himachal Pradesh	1.0	-	-0.40
Jammu & Kashmir	-0.4	-1.24	0.37
Karnataka	0.3	0.97	1.68
Kerala	-0.6	-4.43	-5.41
Madhya Pradesh	-0.1	-0.68	0.48
Maharashtra	3.0	4.1	1.34

Orissa	-0.7	-1.26	-0.55
Punjab	1.7	1.27	0.77
Rajasthan	-0.6	-0.93	-1.34
Tamil Nadu	-0.7	-1.42	4.92
Uttar Pradesh	-2.0	-3.1	-1.94
West Bengal	0.4	1.34	-0.50

Source: Col. 2 Census of India, 2001, Col 3 NSSO-64 & Col. 4 Estimated from Census 2011.

The internal migration data are presented in census report population mobility in the country is marked with significant variations across the states. From the table below we present the pattern of sex wise internal migration in India (2001). From these tables we know the volume of in-migration and out-migration, rate of in and out-migration share of in and out-migration for males and females separately. According, to 1991 census, 5164594 males and 5754389 females crossed the state boundary. This indicates the predominance of female mobility over male mobility in India. The sex ratio among migrants thus comes to 90 males per 100 females. Thus, inter state migration is more female selective.

From the data the rate of in-migration from other states by total as well as sex-wise. Here we see that, Arunachal Pradesh, Goa, Haryana, Maharashtra, Uttaranchal,

Table 18: Sex ratio of in-migration and out migration – India, 1991 and 2001 (males per 100 females)

States	1991		2001	
	Sex ratio of in migrants	Sex ratio of out migrants	Sex ratio of in migrants	Sex ratio of out migrants
India	89.75	89.75	102.12	102.2
Andhra Pradesh	71.60	79.23	77.26	84.69
Arunachal Pradesh	148.86	97.79	140.38	108.58

Assam	134.15	105.02	111.07	81.25
Bihar	49.19	132.91	25.94	16792
Jharkhand	N A	N A	66.70	88.96
Gao	109.98	72.07	124.74	81.89
Gujarat	116.44	75.74	160.25	81.69
Haryana	68.80	53.75	87.75	53.68
Himachal Pradesh	117.80	93.11	132.57	89.75
Jammu & Kashmir	N A	108.52	106.95	93.23
Karnataka	87.09	70.88	100.46	81.31
Kerala	115.54	108.39	117.44	99.82
Madya Pradesh	72.17	54.06	62.95	69.81
Chhattisgarh	N A	N A	83.19	82.87
Maharashtra	114.81	72.45	146.92	76.53
Manipur	171.16	103.77	113.34	123.14
Meghalaya	126.22	77.89	117.62	83.51
Mizoram	200.20	94.47	186.56	108.38
Nagaland	198.85	97.58	161.17	45.24
Orissa	71.70	102.26	82.71	137.12
Punjab	87.94	76.67	120.31	68.65
Rajasthan	59.33	77.17	67.39	87.08
Sikkim	130.24	72.41	133.66	96.75
Tamil Nadu	80.62	106.73	91.38	107.13
Tripura	98.99	80.10	100.77	103.24
Uttar Pradesh	52.18	115.42	58.49	129.77
Uttaranchal	N A	NA	98.79	85.82
West Bengal	100.34	74.13	100.33	111.87
A&N Island	134.40	78.73	128.73	83.68
Chandigarh	114.96	87.36	122.68	92.82
Delhi	199.73	63.24	128.94	77.02

SUBSISTENCE AND DEVELOPMENT MIGRATION

Migration has important economic consequences, both for the actual migrants and for the parental households and villages, depending on the type of migration. Broadly a distinction may be made between subsistence or distress migration and development migration. In the former, the people move out in search of work to survive. It includes many construction workers, road building workers, and other unskilled and semi-skilled laborers. The economic gains of such migration are not sufficient to break the subsistence line. At best it might help migrants to buy food out of their savings to survive during months of unemployment. Secondly, migration under conditions of distress tends to be unstable, and this is so more because of conditions of employment rather than of any inherent love of the worker for his native village. Often workers are recruited on a contract basis only for a period of three to six months by the employers, especially in the category of small scale and medium scale industries. They do so to avoid payment of bonus and other benefits that they must pay if they were to recruit the workers on a more permanent basis. Lack of strong unionization of such workers and inadequate labor laws only convert potential stable labor force into a floating one.

The only exception to this can be seen in Tamil Nadu and West Bengal. A low rate of migration has long been the characteristic feature of Tamil Nadu. In West Bengal, migration rate that was higher than the nation's average till 1971 has registered a drastic decline after that particularly during the 1980s so much so that the rate became one of the lowest in the country in 1991. The backward states generally report a lower percentage of migrants in the population. For instance, Bihar and Uttar Pradesh have reported consistently lower migration rates than the nation's average.

The notable exceptions in this case are Himachal Pradesh and Madhya Pradesh. Among the backward states, these two states have displayed a consistently higher share of inter-state migrants. Thus, a part of the high rate of migration in these two states can be attributed to high rate of inter-state migration, which could possibly be explained in terms of massive public sector investments in the early years resulting in creation of job opportunities. Local population could not take advantage of these developments due to their low level of literacy and skill leaving the door wide open for the migrants from other states (Kundu and Gupta, 2002:266). The other backward states like Orissa and Rajasthan, however, report rates very close to the nation's average.

The rates of migration have undergone decline in all the major states between 1981 and 1991, except in Kerala and Punjab, where the same has registered a marginal increase. The largest decline has been witnessed in Maharashtra – from over 42 per cent in 1981 to around 32 per cent in 1991. The states of Tamil Nadu, Orissa and Bihar are other states where the decline in migration rate is larger than that in the nation's average. This deceleration in the mobility rate is also reflected in the changing proportion of inter-censal migrants between 1981 and 1991. On the eve of the 1981 census, over 40 per cent of the internal migrants were classified as 'inter-censal' migrants. This share has reportedly come down to 35.84 per cent at the time of the 1991 census.

This is indicative of further slowing down of migration during the 1980s. Remarkably, the share of inter-censal migration in urban areas has recorded a sharper decline than that in the rural areas. However, it should be noted that the decline in the share of inter-censal migration in 1991 could not be attributed solely to slowing down of internal migration in the 1980s. As seen in Table 10.3, a part of the decline appears to be related to a larger share of migrants who did not reveal the duration of stay at the time of 1991 census than that of 1981.

The share of inter-censal migrants has undergone a consistent decline in all the major states, though in varying magnitude. Relatively developed states like Maharashtra, Tamil Nadu, Haryana and Andhra Pradesh have witnessed a larger decline than that in the nation's average. Interestingly, backward states like Bihar, Himachal Pradesh, Orissa, and Rajasthan have also witnessed a decline in the share of inter-censal migrants by an equally larger magnitude.

The dynamics of internal migration can best be understood in terms of changes in the share of inter-state migration over time. It has been found that the present level of population mobility across states has considerably declined during the recent past (Kundu and Gupta, 2002:263). The census data of 1981 reveals that of the total internal migrations in the country, about 12 per cent were reported to have moved across state boundaries. Over the period of ten years, this share has gone down by as much as 43 per cent.

States like Andhra Pradesh, Bihar, Karnataka, Kerala, Maharashtra, Orissa, Rajasthan, Tamil Nadu, and West Bengal have all experienced decline in the proportion of inter-state migration between 1981 and 1991. Some scholars attribute this decline to various developmental programs launched by respective state governments during recent decades. People who used to out-migrate in search of jobs are now increasingly being absorbed in their own states. It is also suggested that the growing availability of education, health and other services in relatively less developed states has resulted in a decline in inter-state migration during recent years. Improvement in transport facilities has also minimized the need of moving out, as commuting has become increasingly easier. However, evidence indicate that inter-state inequality in various social and economic indicators of development has sharpened during the recent times, which should have promoted migration across different states.

Table 19: Rate and share of in-migration and out-migration (Total) – India 2001.

States	Total in-migrants from other states	Total out-migrants to other states	Total Population	Rate of in migration	Rate of out migration	Share of total in migrats	Share of total Out migrants
India	1657633	1657633				100.0	100.0
Andhra Pradesh	420981	627958	75727541	0.56	0.83	2.54	3.79
Arunachal Pradesh	71776	12471	1091117	6.58	1.14	0.43	0.08
Assam	121781	280867	26638407	0.46	1.05	0.73	1.69
Bihar	460346	2225514	82878796	0.56	2.69	2.78	13.43
Jharkhand	502723	613761	26909428	1.87	2.28	3.03	3.70
Goa	120626	32274	1343998	8.98	2.40	0.73	0.19
Gujarat	1120284	431741	50596992	2.21	0.85	6.76	2.60
Haryana	1231358	587533	21082989	5.84	2.79	7.43	3.54
H P	188203	165609	6077248	3.10	2.73	1.14	1.00
J & K	86760	122048	10069917	0.86	1.21	0.52	0.74
Karnataka	877437	766483	52733958	1.66	1.45	5.29	4.62
Kerala	230828	421279	31838619	0.72	1.32	1.39	2.54
M P	814570	840317	60385118	1.35	1.39	4.91	5.07
Chhattisgarh	338772	443875	20795956	1.63	2.13	2.04	2.68
Maharashtra	3229733	877169	96752247	3.34	0.91	19.48	5.29
Manipur	4527	30825	2388634	0.19	1.29	0.03	0.19
Meghalaya	33705	20405	2306069	1.46	0.88	0.20	0.12
Mizoram	22598	31724	891058	2.54	3.56	0.14	0.19
Nagaland	33574	51817	1988636	1.69	2.61	0.20	0.31
Orissa	229610	436327	36706920	0.63	1.19	1.39	2.63
Punjab	810916	500986	24289296	3.34	2.06	4.89	3.02
Rajasthan	723416	991882	56473122	1.28	1.76	4.36	5.98

Sikkim	22457	6227	540493	4.15	1.15	0.14	0.04
Tamil Nadu	243387	589547	62110839	0.39	0.95	1.47	3.56
Tripura	40262	23495	3191168	1.26	0.74	0.24	0.14
U P	1078751	3791774	166052859	0.65	2.28	6.51	22.87
Uttaranchal	352379	353862	8479562	4.16	4.17	2.13	2.13
W B	724396	726865	80221171	0.90	0.91	4.37	4.38
A&N island	29442	7856	356265	8.26	2.21	0.18	0.05
Chandigarh	239227	106674	906914	26.55	11.84	1.44	0.64
Delhi	2171453	457068	13782976	15.75	3.32	13.10	2.76

Development migration, on the contrary, is characterized by a higher level of skills, training, and education of the migrants. Such migrants qualify for more remunerative jobs. In many cases migrants will have to leave behind their wives, children, and their parents. They send money home for the maintenance of their dependents, and this gives rise to a money order economy resulting in developmental activities. The native family will be able to clear off loans and debts, build houses, eat good food and wear decent clothes. Besides this general improvement in the standard of life, in some cases, where the remittances are significant, as in the case of migrants from Punjab and Gujarat villages, the natal families invest in modern agricultural technology, small scale industries and establish educational institutions.

The development effects of another category of migrants who are engaged in trade, commerce and industry prove highly impressive. Many Marwaris who have migrated to towns and cities in different parts of India, save up substantial amounts of money which are not only reinvested in their business but also in philanthropic activities in hometowns and villages, by building temples, hospitals, establishing educational trusts and institutions, and running eye operation camps. Kundu and Gupta (2002) have, therefore, argued that a better explanation for increasing immobility in India can be found in terms of growing assertion of regional identity, education (up to high school) in regional languages, adoption of Master Plans and land use restrictions at the city level etc. All these factors, directly or indirectly, discourage migration. In addition, according to them, decline in inter-state migration can also be attributed to widening intra-state inequality among backward states and growing absorption of prospective migrants in select large cities usually state capitals.

They argue that in backward states, the state capitals emerged as centers of industrial investment because they already enjoyed the advantage of industrial base and a high level of basic services. These centers attracted a large chunk of the subsidized amenities while the other areas received very little of the same. Consequently, the intra-state inequality sharpened resulting in increased migration of people from backward regions or districts to large cities within the same state. Geographers have traditionally been interested in the net impact of migration on population growth at regional levels. Census data on migration enable us to derive estimates on net migration for states and union territories. Based on 'birthplace' data scholars have identified the 'gaining' or 'losing' states in the country during individual decades in the post-independence period. Their findings suggest that although the pattern of gaining and losing states underwent change from one decade to another, states like Maharashtra and Gujarat consistently appeared as the gaining states while Uttar Pradesh, Bihar and Andhra Pradesh have lost population throughout the period (Bhende and Kanitkar, 2000:370-71). Using the 'place of last residence' data on lifetime migrants of 1991 census, this author has worked out the net migration in fifteen major states in the country.

The results are summarized in Table. As is seen in the table, states like Gujarat, Haryana, Karnataka, Madhya Pradesh, Maharashtra, and West Bengal have gained in their population through migration. In terms of the share of net inter-state migration in the total population of the state, Maharashtra occupies the first place in the country, followed by Madhya Pradesh and West Bengal. Remarkably, all the gaining states, except Madhya Pradesh, are relatively developed states. However, Punjab and Tamil Nadu are exceptions to this.

These states have instead experienced loss in their population through inter-state migration. Along with Punjab and Tamil Nadu, other states, which are reported to have lost population. through more out-migration than in-migration, include Andhra Pradesh, Bihar, Himachal Pradesh, Kerala, Orissa, Rajasthan, and Uttar Pradesh. It should be noted that barring Andhra Pradesh, all other states are relatively backward states. Most of them have been characteristically out-migrating states for quite some time now. In Bihar and Uttar Pradesh, the losses in population are of the magnitude of 1.99 million and 3.88 million respectively.

Table 20 : Inter-State net Migration in Major States of India,1991 (based on 'place of last residence' criterion')

States	Interstate In-migrants	Interstate Out-migrants	Net Migration
Andhra Pradesh	994141	1226447	-232306
Bihar	1031566	3234991	-1991425
Gujarat	1465214	935402	529812
Haryana	1579052	1425974	153078
Himachal Pradesh	236830	293344	-56314
Karnataka	1600231	1426629	173602
Kerala	437087	968941	-531854
Madhya Pradesh	2457392	1486390	971102
Maharashtra	4059626	1772508	2287118
Orissa	592596	621508	-28909
Punjab	1120282	1376312	-256030
Rajasthan	1470102	1951942	-481745
Tamil Nadu	842996	1465861	-622865
Uttar Pradesh	1873515	5753997	3882482
West Bengal	2005331	1119915	885416

Source: Census of India 1991, Migration Tables.

OTHER CONSEQUENCES OF MIGRATION

Migration tends to be selective not only based on age and sex but also based on caste, religion, language, region. Village and kinship ties. Normally, a single adult male moves in search of job to a town, secures one, and he in turn gets his friends and kinsfolk. In course of time a settlement based on language, kin, caste, and region comes into being. Such settlements help create a situation of cultural pluralism, for the migrants from a particular region establish voluntary associations in a bid to recreate their home culture and to fight for the necessities of urban life such as housing and education. They also provide security to the fresh immigrants and act as 'brokers. Such favorable conditions of living in the place of destination attract more migrants on the one hand and make the migrant population more stable, on the other.

A substantial portion of the migrants live as squatters in slums developing cultural identity of their own and a community life based on it. Housing is cheap as it only means erecting another hut on the vacant plot. The area gets overcrowded and in the absence of any civic amenities slumming conditions get worse day-by-day. The city administration takes the view that the hutment dwellers are squatters, hence, it is not their responsibility to provide drainage, sewerage, water, electricity, and garbage clearance services. However, it is necessary to take a sympathetic view of the hutment dwellers. In the absence of any program on the part of the state to house the low-income group, the slums do provide an answer to their economic, social, and cultural needs. Hence, development or clearance of slums becomes a necessary sequel to the immigration of the unskilled or semi-skilled workers.

Instead of thinking of solutions after the slums have come into existence, any sound planning should consider measure of checking and controlling them. For instance, when the state establishes an industrial estate or a wholesale market, the housing of the laborer's should form part of planning with all the urban infrastructure. Migration to metropolitan cities will have to be controlled and regulated at the very initial stage. We should have enough information about the migrants: their identity in terms of employment, residence, places from which they have migrated, reasons for migration, local contacts, age, sex, skills, etc. This will help assess the state of unemployment among migrants with specific categories of skills, the directions of migration inflow, the demands made on housing, transport, communication, and social welfare. A welfare state has to operate on these lines assuming all the responsibilities.

URBAN AREA DEVELOPMENT

An effective way of controlling indiscriminate migration is to plan develop the region, especially the metropolitan region, in terms of which there has already been a good deal of thinking. The industries need to be dispersed; adequate transport and communications will have to be provided. Even there is no escape from having a massive program of establishing housing estates for the industrial workers and laborer's, vendors and hawkers, and shack stall holders who follow the industries, markets, and residential colonies. In the absence of a comprehensive plan the problem of indiscriminate migration and the consequent slum development will only get displaced but not solved.

The national capital region (Delhi) plan suggests dispersal of industries, administration and other activities and conceives of the settlement system in terms of seventeen growth centers. However, the problem is not so much the diversion of migrants by providing counter magnates and growth points but to handle the concomitant problems of new slums, new unauthorized colonies, shack-shop complexes and new problems of crime, law, and order. Hence, dispersal of industries and other economic activities alone will not lead to urban development. The central issue to me is to plan settlement of 60,000 migrants who pour into Delhi from rural areas every year, and who largely belong to the informal sector of the economy.

Another important aspect of urban development is the development of the inhabited areas of the villages in the metropolitan region. At present, in the name of not disturbing the villagers, the inhabited area is reduced to a slum-island during developed areas. This policy needs to be re-developed with all the urban infrastructure. In fact, it should be considered as another means of providing compensation to the villages whose land will have been acquired for development purposes. Further, the villages on the fringe of a metropolitan city or an industrial town are found to receive an influx of immigrant workers because of several advantages such as cheap housing, nearness to work and cheaper cost of living. Over a period, the fringe villages become over-crowded and will be reduced to slums. Hence, the necessity of providing the urban infrastructure to prevent slumming conditions.

Any urban area development plan should consider city, towns and villages as functionally differentiated but inter-related. The villages with irrigational facilities should be encouraged to develop market gardening, dairy, and poultry farming. Such villages not only provide the greenbelt for the metropolis but also act as a feeder belt supplying the commodities necessary for the city dwellers. Such developmental activities will also attract migrants who would have otherwise flocked to the city. Rural development is complementary to urban development; it helps dispersal of migrants.

Urban area development may take diverse patterns. The metropolitan area development may be conceived in terms of twin cities as in Bombay or satellite towns with the city at the centers as in Delhi and Madras. The conurbation should take the pattern which is best suited for the ecological and economic conditions of the region. Another pattern of regional development, in the absence of a metropolitan focus, is to provide multiple but interconnected foci. An aspect of the urban fringe development is the planning of the commuters' zone. People not only commute from villages and towns to the city but also from city to outskirts where industries are located. Thus, commuting is both centripetal and centrifugal. Efficient and quick mass transport is a pre-requisite in dispersal of settlements and avoiding congestion in the urban area.

In this context, development of smaller urban complexes including small and medium size towns needs to be stressed. For instance, Hospet-Bellary region in Karnataka has such a growth potential. Hospet has emerged as a mining town with manganese mines all around. Part of the region is canal irrigated and has become another tice bowl of Karnataka. Hospet is also a tourist center with the ruins on Vijayanagar Empire and the Tungabhadra dam site. Bellary, which is about forty miles from Hospet is the center of trade and commerce, education and administration.

With such a diversified but functionally related economic activities the area has all the potential for the development of small urban region.

Planning of small urban regions serves two important purposes. First, it helps the small towns, which are now decaying, grow. Secondly, it will divert the flow of migration to metropolitan centers thus bringing about balanced urban growth in the country.

Table 21: Trends in Urbanization in India (1901-2011)

Year	Number of Urban Agglomeration town	Total Population (in Million)	Urban population (in million)	Rural Population (in Million)
1901	1927	238.39	25,85	212.54
1911	1825	252.09	25.94	226.15
1921	1949	251.32	28.08	223.23
1931	2072	270.97	33.45	245.52
1941	2250	318.66	44.15	274.50

1951	2843	361.08	62.44	298.64
1961	2363	439.23	78.93	360.29
1971	2590	598.15	109.11	489.04
1981	3378	683.32	159.46	523.86
1991	3768	844.32	217.17	627.14
2001	5161	1027.02	285.35	741.66
2011	7935	1210.57	377.10	833.46

Source: Census of India, various reports.

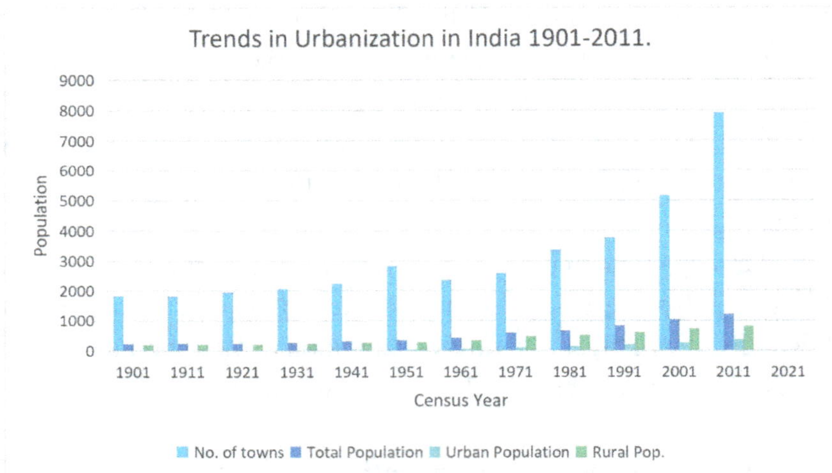

Chapter III

DRIFT IN POPULATION OF KARNATAKA:

Urbanization is crucially linked to migration. Whether migration is a strong or a weak force in the urbanization process depends upon the nature and pattern of migration. Apart from economic reasons, migration occurs due to a host of socio-cultural and other factors. Before the contribution of migration in urban growth is discussed, it would be worthwhile to mention the nature and source of migration data in India.

The size of India's population has been one of its distinguishing features. At the 1971 census, the population of India was 547,949,809 consisting of 283,936,614 males and 264,013,195 females. The population of Karnataka state, as on the reference date of the 1971 census , is 29,299,014 persons made up of 14,971,900 males and 14,327,114 females. Karnataka state thus contributes 5.35% of the country's population. It is interesting to consider the population of this state in comparison with that of the other states and union territories. Karnataka state is eighth both in area and population among the states in India. It accounts for 5.35% of the country's population.

Distribution of population among the districts:

The study of the distribution of population is important because this would indicate the way in which the population is arranged within the area available for exploitation and settlement. People use land for agriculture, forestry, mining, manufacturing, commerce, and housing and, in so using the area available, they create patterns of distribution that reflect the adjustments with environment and resources. This spatial distribution of population can be viewed from different angles such as differentials densities of settlement, rural-urban concentrations, distribution with reference to natural resources, etc. However, the distribution of population can also be considered from the point of view of specific administrative units. A consideration of the distribution of population by districts and talukas gives a broad picture of the population profile of the state.

The average population of a district in the state is 1,542,053. Bangalore district has the highest population of 3,365,515, which is more than double the district average. The average district population is also exceeded by the districts of Belgaum (2,423,342), Dharwad (2,342,213), Mysore (2,077,238), Bijapur (1,985,591), South Kanara (1,939,315), Gulbarga (1,739,220) and Tumkur (1,627,721). Of these eight districts with populations higher than the average district population, the districts of Belgaum, Bijapur, Dharwad and Gulbarga are contiguous and lie in the Northern Maidan area of the state. Similarly, in the Southern part of the state, Bangalore, and Tumkur districts are contiguous.

The least populated district is Coorg with a population of 378,291, which is far below the average district population. The other districts with populations lower than that of the average district population are Chikamagalur (736,647), Bidar (824,059), North Kanara (849,105), Hassan (1,102,370), Bellary (1,122,686), Mandya (1,154,374), Shimoga (1,301,485), Chitra Durga (1,397,456), Raichur (1,415,740), and Kolar (1,516,646). The population of the districts of Coorg, Chickamagalur, Bidar and North Kanara are less than one million. Coorg, Hassan, Mandya, Chickmagalur, Shimoga and North Kanara form one block, the districts being contiguous to each other. Similarly, Bellary, Chitradurga and Raichur districts constitute one block. The districts in the state are of different areas and their contributions both in terms of population and area to the population and area of the state vary widely. The proportion of population attributable to each district, the rank it takes in the population and area scales, with a comparison with 1961 are indicated in Table 10.

The districts of Bijapur, Gulbarga and Raichur which have the first three ranks on the area scale, have fairly lower ranks on the population scale. The largest district, Bijapur, has the 5th place in terms of population, while Gulbarga and Raichur have the 7th and 8th ranks, respectively. The districts of Bengaluru, Belgaum, Dharwad, Mysore, South Kanara, Kolar, Mandaya and Hassan have ranks on the population scale higher than what they have on the area scale. Tumkur, Bidar and Coorg districts have the same ranks both in terms of area and population. Coorg district occupies the lowest tank both in area and population. It is interesting to notice that the districts occupy same ranks on the population-scale that they had in 1961 except in the case of Bellary and Mandya.

TABLE 10 : Ranks of districts in terms of population and area

Rank in population.	Name of district	Proportion of population of state (%)	Proportion of area of state (%)	Rank area	Rank in population in 1961
1	Bengaluru	11.49	4.17	14	1
2	Belgaum	8.27	6.99	5	2
3	Dharwad	7.99	7.17	4	3
4	Mysuru	7.09	6.23	6	4
5	Bijapur	6.78	8.89	1	5
6	South Kanara	6.62	4.40	12	6
7	Gulbarga	5.94	8.46	2	7
8	Tumkur	5.56	5.53	8	8
9	Kolar	5.18	4.29	13	9
10	Raichur	4.83	7.30	3	10
11	Chitradurga	4.77	5.66	7	11
12	Shimoga	4.44	5.50	9	12
13	Mandya	3.94	2.59	18	13
14	Bellary	3.83	5.16	11	14
15	Hassan	3.76	3.56	16	15
16	North Kanara	2.90	5.36	10	16

17	Bidar	2.81	2.84	17	17
18	Chickmagalur	2.51	3.76	15	18
19	Coorg	1.29	2.14	19	19

In 1961, Bellary had the 13th place and Mandya the 14th but in 1971, these districts have interchanged ranks, with Bellary now 14th and Mandaya 13th. The average area of a district in the state is 10,093 sq.km. of the 19 districts in the state, the 10 districts of Belgaum, Bijapur, Chitradurga, Dhawar, Gulbarga, Mysore, North Kanara, Raichur, Shimoga and Tumkur have areas greater than the average area of district, while the other 9 districts have areas smaller than the average area of a district.

TABLE 11: Density of population of the districts

Name of Districts	Density of population (per sq.km.)				
	Total		Rural		Urban
	1971	1961	1971	1961	1971
Mysore state	153	123	118	97	2272
Bangalore	421	310	193	153	7605
Belgaum	181	149	148	124	1221
Bellary	113	93	85	73	1185
Bidar	151	123	131	108	2157
Bijapur	116	98	95	81	729
Chickmagalur	102	82	87	70	2861
Chitradurga	129	101	103	84	5071
Coorg	92	78	79	68	1404
Dhawar	170	142	122	107	1338
Gulbarga	107	86	88	73	4738
Hassan	162	129	141	115	3161
Kolar	184	157	148	123	3175
Mandya	233	185	204	167	2331
Mysore	174	142	131	108	3815

North Kanara	83	67	68	56	2048
Raichur	101	78	86	68	2451
Shimoga	123	97	95	73	5752
South Kanara	230	192	188	160	1897
Tumkur	153	130	136	117	3127

Density of population:

The density of population is the number of persons per sq.km. The population of Mysore state as recorded at the 1971 census is 29,299,014 persons and its area is 191,773 sq. km. The density of population of the state is, therefore, 153 persons per sq.km. The density in 1961 was 123 persons per sq.km. The density of population of the districts is indicated in Table 2.2. This statement indicates the density for all areas and for rural and urban areas separately. For comparison, the corresponding data for 1961 are also available.

The highest density is in Bangalore and the lowest in North Kanara district. The density in the other districts range between these limits and there are considerable differences between district and district. The districts can be arranged on the basis of their densities above or below the state average as follows: Tumkur district has a density equal to the state average of 153.

Table12: District rank for State Average.

Districts with density above state average			Districts with density below state average	
(State average 153)				
1	Bangalore	421	1	Bidar
2	Mandya	233	2	Chitradurga
3	South Kanara	230	3	Shimoga
4	Kolar	184	4	Bijapur
5	Belgaum	181	5	Bellary
6	Mysore	174	6	Gulbarga

7	Dhawar	170	7	Chickmagalur
8	Hassan	162	8	Raichur
			9	Coorg
			10	North Kanara

The rural density is highest in Mandya and least in North Kanara district. The districts can be arranged based on rural densities being above or below the state average as follows:

Table 13: Districts ranked by rural density.

Districts with rural density above state average			Districts with rural density below state average	
(State average 118)				
1	Mandya	204	1	Chitradurga
2	Bangalore	193	2	Bijapur
3	Southkanara	188	3	Shimoga
4	Belgaum	148	4	Gulbarga
5	Kolar	148	5	Chickmagalur
6	Hassan	141	6	Raichur
7	Tumkur	136	7	Bellary
8	Bidar	131	8	Coorg
9	Mysore	131	9	North Kanara
10	Dharwad	122		

The highest urban density is in Bangalore district, the concentration being in Bangalore city, and the lowest urban density is in Bijapur district. The districts can be arranged based on urban districts above or below the state average as follows:

Table 14: Districts ranked by Urban Density.

Districts with urban density above state average (State average 2272)			Districts with urban density below state average	
1	Bangalore	7605	1	Bidar
2	Shimoga	5752	2	North Kanara
3	Chitradurga	5071	3	South Kanara
4	Gulbarga	4738	4	Coorg
5	Mysore	3815	5	Dharwad
6	Kolar	3175	6	Belgaum
7	Hassan	3161	7	Bellary
8	Tumkur	3127	8	Bijapur
9	Chickmagalur	2861		
10	Raichur	2451		
11	Mandya	2331		

The changes in densities between 1961 and 1971 are interesting. In 1961 the densities were below 100 in three groups of districts: the 1st group consisting of Hijapur, Gulbarga, Raichur, Bellary, the 2nd group consisting of North Kanara, Shimoga, Chickmagalur; and the 3rd group consisting of Coorg only. In 1971, the districts in the 1st group, namely, Bijapur, Gulbarga, Raichur and Bellary had moved upon the density scale and crossed 100 sq. km. but of the districts in the 2nd group only Shimoga and Chickmagalur crossed a density of 100, the increase in Shimoga being particularly high. North Kanara and Coorg districts, even in 1971, have densities below 100, though higher than those in 1961. Tumkur and Hassan districts, which had densities below 140 in 1961, have now crossed 150. Belgaum, Dhawar and Kolar districts, which were above the state average density in 1961 and comparatively high-density areas in 1961, continues to be so in 1971 also. The districts of Bangalore, Mandaya and South Kanara were, in 1961, in the higher density ranges. They continue to be so in 1971 also. Bidar district has also increased in density.

In a few cases, there is an apparent fall in the urban densities in 1971 from that in 1961. This is due to methods of computation of density in the case of urban areas. (Urban areas include places constituted into municipalities, cantonments, or other statutory areas where the areas of the built-up portions and total jurisdiction are clearly known, and also town panchayats or large villages declared as towns. In the case of town panchayats and large villages declared as towns, the population is usually concentrated in a gaothana or village core, the rest of the area being agricultural lands, but the area of the built-up portion is not known and the only area data available relate to the entire area of the village within its revenue limits). The use of such large areas naturally lowers the density in such cases.

The total number of rural to urban migrants is 307,189 of which 1961,286 or 52.50% are males and 145,903 or 47.50% are females. In terms of absolute number, the rural to urban migration within the state but outside the district of birth is much smaller than the rural-to-rural migration within the state but outside the district of birth. However, such a migration is one of the most important factors that influence urban population growth. In the case of most of the districts, the male out-numbers females indicating that this type of migration is due to economic reasons. The largest proportion of rural to urban migrants consists of those who have moved from their villages and lived in towns for a duration of 1 to 5 years. The next large groups are in the duration of 15 years and above. In the periods of duration of migration of 6-10 years, 11-15 years, and 16 years and over, females exceed males, indicating the influence of migration consequent on marriage. In the shorter durations of less than one year and 1-5 years, males exceed females since the former migrate due to economic reasons.

Of the 307,189 migrants from rural areas of one district to urban areas of another district, 80,806 have moved into the urban areas of

Bangalore district. This is clearly the result of the pull exerted by the Metropolitan area of Bangalore. The general pattern is that in the longer durations of such migration, the number of females exceeds that of the males, however, in Bangalore district, the number of males is greater than the number of females for all periods of duration of migration indicating the large influx into the Metropolitan Area of Bangalore of males. For every 10,000 persons enumerated in the rural areas, 2,263 males and 5214 females have been born outside the place of enumeration but within the district while 608 males and 919 females have been born in other districts of the state. Thus, those born within the same district far out-number those born in other districts. Migration is, therefore, more prominent within the same districts than from district to district. The migration within the districts is also largely from one rural area in the district to another. Out of the 2,263 males who are born within the district but outside the place of enumeration, 2,108 are from rural areas and 150 from urban areas. Among the 5,124 females who are born within the district but outside the place of enumeration, 4,966 belong to the rural areas and 240 are from the urban areas. The migration within the district is mostly rural to rural. The migration from the urban to the rural is only slight. This is understandable as the rural pull is less than the rural push. The rural migration is mostly for social and other reasons, the economic reasons while no doubt present, are not so strong. The larger proportion of female migration is due to marriages only. Of those born outside the district, the larger proportions are again from the rural areas, the urban component being very small.

For every 10,000 persons enumerated in the urban areas 2,000 males and 2,836 females are born elsewhere in the district of enumeration, while 1,518 males and 1,469 females are born in other districts of the state. The difference in proportions between the males born elsewhere in the district and those born in other districts of the state is not very much indicating that the urban pull operates fairly uniformly. Of those born outside the place of enumeration but within the districts, the majority are from the rural areas of the district. Out of the 2,000 males 1,416 are from the rural areas and 503 from the urban areas. Out of the 2,336 females, 1,674 are from the rural areas and 660 from the urban areas. Of those born in other districts of the state, the distribution between rural and urban areas is largely similar.

Coorg district has the highest % of inter-district immigration to the population of the district. However, in absolute numbers, this is less than that of Bangalore district. There is a net accretion to the population of the district, taking into consideration both in and out migration, in the districts of Bangalore, Chickmagalur, Chitra Durga, Coorg, Dhawar, Gulbarga, Hassan, Mandya, North Kanara and Shimoga. In the other districts, migration has resulted in a net decrease in the total population of the district. There is a constant movement of population between the various states of India. The total number of immigrants of Karnataka state from other states is 10,40,331 while the emigrants from this state to other state number 794,110. Thus, immigrants exceed emigrants by 246,221. Madras contributes the largest proportion of the immigrants with 38.13% of the total immigrants being from that state. The next largest proportion of 27.98% is from Andhra Pradesh followed by Maharashtra state with 16.27% and Kerala with 13.19%. Thus, 95.57% of the immigrants into Mysore state are from the neighboring four states. The contribution from the Northern states is marginal, the largest being 1.24% from Rajasthan.

The emigration from Karnataka to other states indicates that the largest proportion of emigrants goes to Maharashtra. Of the emigrants from the state, 58.96% go to Maharashtra. The next largest proportion of 23.07% go to Andhra Pradesh. Madras receives 11.17% of the emigrants and Kerala only 2.69%. Thus, 95.87% of the emigrants go to the four neighboring states. The proportion that emigrants North is very small. The immigrants from Madras exceed the emigrants from Karnataka by 308,007. Those from Kerala exceed the emigrants to Kerala by 115,834 while in the case of Andhra Pradesh the difference is 107,904. In the case of Maharashtra, the emigrants from Karnataka exceed the immigrants from Maharashtra by 298,923. In the case of the states of Andhra Pradesh, Gujarat, Kerala, Madras, Punjab, Rajasthan and Uttar Pradesh, the number who come into Karnataka state exceed those that migrates from this state. In the case of the states of Assam, Bihar, Jammu and Kashmir, Madhya Pradesh, Maharashtra, Orissa and West Bengal, the numbers that leave Karnataka from these states exceed the number of those coming into the former from the latter.

Of the 10,40,331 migrants from other states into Karnataka state, 505,088 have migrated to the rural areas and 535,246 to the urban areas of the state, i.e., of the total migrants from other states, 48.55% have migrated to the rural areas and 51.45% to the urban areas of this state. Of the migrants from the various states, the greater proportion (66.83%) of migrants in the case of Maharashtra move into the rural areas. Among the migrants from Madras, 64.68% move into the urban areas. In the case of Andhra Pradesh, the greater proportion move into the rural areas. Among the migrants who come from the other states, and move into the rural areas of Karnataka state, the largest proportion is from Andhra Pradesh (34.11%). The next largest proportion of migrants to the rural areas is from Madras (27.14%). Kerala contributes 22.39% and Maharashtra 14.47%. In fact, 98.71% of the migrants from other states who migrates to the rural areas of this state are from Andhra Pradesh, Kerala, Madras and Maharashtra. Among those from other states who migrates into the urban areas of Karnataka state, 47.93% are from Madras, 22.19% from Andhra Pradesh, 11.97% from Kerala and 10.49% from Maharashtra. Thus, 92.58% of the migrants from other states who migrate into the urban areas of Karnataka are from these four states.

Of the 172,280 migrants from Andhra Pradesh who migrate to the rural areas of Karnataka state, the larger number are found in the districts of Bellary, Bidar, Chitradurga, Gulbarga, Kolar, Raichur,

Shimoga and Tumkur. In other words, 93.73% of the migrants from Andhra Pradesh into the rural areas of Karnataka State are in these eight districts. The large numbers in the rural parts of Bellary and Raichur move in for agricultural work. This is true of the other districts also. Of the migrants from Andhra Pradesh to the urban areas in Karnataka, the larger proportions are in the districts of Bangalore, Bellary, Kolar, Raichur and Shimoga. The largest number is in Bangalore district. Of those from Kerala who have migrated to the rural areas of this state, the larger proportions are in the districts of Chickmagalur, Coorg and South Kanara. They have migrated into these districts mainly as plantation labor. Of those from Kerala who have migrated to the urban areas of the state, the majority are found in the districts of Bangalore, Coorg, Shimoga and South Kanara.

Of those from Maharashtra who have migrated to the rural areas of Karnataka state, the larger proportions are in the districts of Belgaum, Bidar, Bijapur, Gulbarga and North Kanara. Of those from Maharashtra who have migrated to the urban areas of this state, the larger proportions are in the districts of Belgaum, Bijapur, Bangalore, Dhawar and Gulbarga.

Among those from the neighboring states migrating to the urban areas of Karnataka state, the majority moves into Bangalore district from the state of Andhra Pradesh, Kerala and Madras. In the case of those from Maharashtra, the largest proportions of such migrants move to the urban areas of Belgaum district. Among those who migrates to the rural areas of the State, those from Kerala are mainly in the plantation areas while those from Madras are distributed over the plantation areas and industrial areas. In the case of those from Andhra Pradesh, the majority of those who migrates to the rural areas of the state are in areas of agricultural activity. Emigrants from Karnataka state to the other states in India is 794,110. These emigrants move either to the rural or urban areas of other states and their distribution is not uniform.

Of the total emigrants from the state, 40.05% have migrated to the rural areas of other states while 59.95% have migrated to the rural areas of other states while 59.95% have migrated to the urban areas of other states. This follows the same characteristic as migration from other states into Karnataka where also the migration to urban areas exceeds that to the rural areas. Except in the case of the states of Andhra Pradesh, Jammu and Kashmir and Kerala where the number migrating from Karnataka to the rural areas of these stat4es is greater, in all the other states, the migration from Karnataka to the urban areas exceeds that to the rural areas of the other states. The emigrants from the rural areas of Karnataka are 477,918 to whom 318,117 of them migrate to the rural areas of other states, or 66.56% of the rural emigrants from Karnataka migrate to the rural areas of other states. The rest, though from rural Karnataka, migrates to the urban areas of other states. Generally, the rural emigration is largely to rural areas of other states and urban emigration is largely to the urban areas of other states. However, in the case of Kerala, some of the urban emigrants from Karnataka migrates to the rural areas of Kerala. But the emigration from rural areas to urban areas of other states is also apparent.

The immigrants from outside the state account for 4.31% of the males and 4.52% of the females. There are a relatively greater proportion of males except in the districts of Belgaum, Bellary, Bidar, Bijapur, Chitradurga, Gulbarga, Kolar, Raichur and Tumkur. Except for Chitradurga district, the other districts mentioned are border districts and the relatively greater proportion of females in these districts among the immigrants is due to marriage migration from the neighboring areas in the adjacent states. In the case of Chitradurga district which border Andhra Pradesh, as will be apparent, there is a high proportion of migrants from Andhra Pradesh and since this group is likely to marry only from their own language group in their home state, the female proportion of immigrants is greater. Bangalore district has a high proportion of male immigration due to the employment opportunities available which would attract immigrants. The districts of Chickmagalur, Coorg and Shimoga have also high proportions of male immigrants because of the plantation labor that migrates from other states to these Malnad areas. Correspondingly, the proportion of female immigration into these districts is comparatively high due to marriage migration.

The actual population of the state is 23,586,772 consisting of 12,040,923 males and 11,545,849 females. If immigrants are excluded and emigrants are included, the result would be the natural population of the state or that population which the state would have had, had there been no migration at all. This natural population is 23,340,551 or 246,221 less than the actual population. Karnataka state receives more people than migrate from it. The actual sex ratio is 959 but the sex ratio on the basis of the natural population is 963. The difference is not significant. Thus, migration does not have any major influence on the sex ratio. The sex ratio of 1,027 in the case of immigrants from the adjacent states indicates that more females than males immigrate from the adjacent states. The sex ratio in the rural areas of such immigrants from the neighboring states is 1,240, while for the urban areas it is 850. The number of females immigrating to the rural areas from the adjacent states exceeds the number of immigrating males while in the case of the urban areas the immigrating males exceed the females. The sex ratio is low in the case of immigrants from states other than the adjacent states.

The sex ratio of 1,203 is favorable to females in the case of emigrants from Karnataka state to the adjacent states. The emigration is largely due to marriage migration. The sex ratio in this case for the urban area is, however, only 963 as against 1,386 for the rural areas. More emigration of females to the adjacent states occurs than of males, from the rural areas of Karnataka than from urban areas. The migration of females to the state other than the adjacent state is low. For every 1,000 males only 611 females emigrate to the state which are not adjacent to Karnataka state. The ratio is 687 for the urban areas and 457 for the rural areas. The emigration of females from the urban areas of the state to states other than adjacent states is greater than the emigration to these states of females from the rural areas of Karnataka.

The immigrants into Karnataka state from other states compared to the language returns for the numerically predominant languages of the respective states. Except in a few cases, the immigrants into the state are less in number than those in Karnataka who speak the predominant language of the state of origin. The difference in the number of migrants and the excess of speakers of the predominant language can be explained since the latter would include all those born in Karnataka state but talking the languages predominant in other states.

The immigration into the rural areas of Karnataka from the rural areas of the adjacent states is very much more prominent than that from the rural areas of states other than the adjacent states. Rural to rural migration is in a sense zonal. The number of rural females exceeds the immigrating males due to marriage migration. However, migration as such contributes only a small proportion to the rural population. Immigration into the rural areas is comparatively higher in the districts of Belgaum, Bellary, Chickmagalur, Coorg, Kolar, Shimoga and South Kanara. The proportion of rural immigrants from the rural areas of the other states to the rural population of the districts is comparatively higher in the districts of Belgaum, Bellary, Bidar, Chickagalur, Coorg, Kolar, North Kanara and Shimoga.

Urban to urban migration in terms of absolute number is highest in Bangalore district. However, for the state immigrants from the urban areas of other states contribute less than 5% of the total urban population of the state. As in the case of rural-to-rural immigration, in the case of urban-to-urban immigration also, the larger numbers are from the adjacent states. The proportion of such immigrants to the urban population is comparatively high in the districts of Bangalore, Bellary, Coorg and Shimoga.

The immigration from other states of India that marriage tends to bring in move female immigrants from the rural areas of other states into the urban areas of this state as the migration period increases. In case of migration from urban areas of other states of India into the urban areas of Karnataka state by duration, the conclusion drawn above regarding migration from rural areas of other states into the urban areas of Karnataka state hold good. For shorter duration of migration, males exceed females but as duration increases the numbers tend to equate. The immigrants under Category-I-cultivation-or-II-agricultural laborers constitutes only small proportions of the total population in these industrial categories. The larger proportions of these immigrants who are cultivators are in the districts of Belgaum, Bellary, Bidar, Coorg, Gulbarga, Kolar and Tumkur. The largest proportion is in Kolar district. Of these immigrants in Category-II-as agricultural laborer's, the larger proportions are in the districts of Belgaum, Bellary, Bidar, Chickmagalur, Chitradurga, Coorg, Gulbarga, Kolar, Mandya, Raichur, Shimoga and Tumkur. The highest proportion is in Coorg district. These districts are all areas of increased agricultural activity including irrigation into Karnataka state as % of the total, rural and urban population of Karnataka.

TABLE 15:Migrants of each sex for different durations of residents from rural areas of other states of India to urban areas of Karnataka state, 1961

	Total Migrants	1 year	1-5 years	6-10 years	11-15 years	16 years and over	Period not states
Karnataka							
P	278382	47343	83005	52172	32945	59840	3077
M	156155	30785	47710	27042	17250	31877	1491
F	122227	16558	35295	25130	15695	27963	1586
P	100.00	17.01	29.82	18.74	11.83	21.49	1.11
M	100.00	19.72	30.55	17.32	11.04	21.41	0.96

F	100.00	13.55	28.87	20.56	12.84	22.88	1.30
P	100.00	100.00	100.00	100.00	100.00	100.00	100.00
M	56.09	65.03	57.48	51.83	52.36	53.27	48.46
F	43.91	34.97	42.52	48.17	47.04	46.73	51.54

Table 16:Migrants from urban areas of other states of India to urban areas of Karnataka state, 1961

	Total Migrants	1 year	1-5 years	6-10 years	11-15 years	16 years and over	Period does not state
Karnataka							
M	133138	23441	46175	23218	13606	24820	1878
F	116533	14622	38772	23490	13870	24810	1970

Immigrants from other states accounts for 4.41% of the population of the state with 4.22% from the adjacent states and only 0.19% from the non-adjacent states. Immigration is largely from the neighboring states. The proportions of male and female immigrants from the adjacent states are similar with a slightly higher proportion of females. But in the case of the non-adjacent states, the proportion of males exceeds that of females. In the case of the former, marriage migration accounts for the high proportion of female immigration while the latter would indicate that with increasing distances, marriage migration gets reduced. The proportion of migration from the adjacent states is very much more than from the states other than the adjacent ones. There is a greater proportion of migration to the urban areas than to the rural areas of Karnataka from the states which are not adjacent.

TABLE 17:

Immigration from other states of India into the state, classified by sex, expressed by % of total, rural and urban population of the state, 1961

Total/ Rural/ Urban	Population of state			Percentage of total immigrants from other states of India to actual population of state	
	Total	Male	Female	Total	Male
Total	23536772	12040923	11545849	4.41	4.31
Rural	18320279	9287660	9032619	2.76	2.44
Urban	5266493	2753263	25132230	10.16	10.63

Among those who have migrated into the state for less than 1 year, the males are far greater in number than the females. This is generally true in the migration period of 1-5 years and indicates that the males migrate in larger numbers for shorter durations due to economic reasons. As the duration increases, the number of females is almost equal to the number of males indicating utilization, digging of wells and soil conservation works.

Table 18: Percentage of Immigrants from States adjacent to the State.

Percentage of immigration from states adjacent to the state to actual population of state			Percentage of immigration from states other than those adjacent to state to actual population of state	
Total	Male	Female	Total	Male
4.22	4.07	4.36	0.19	0.24
2.72	2.40	3.06	0.04	0.04
9.41	9.73	9.06	0.75	0.90

Category III includes those engaged in Mining and Quarrying, livestock, forestry, fishing, hunting and plantations, orchards and allied activities. The proportion of immigrants from other states to the total population engaged in this activity is 20.54%. This is a fairly large proportion. The larger proportions are in the districts of Bellary (35.07%), Chickmagalur (32.98%), Coorg (42.60%), Hassan (26.75%), Kolar (36.04%), North Kanara (10.58%), Raichur (22.93%) and Shimoga (19.10%). The main activity in the districts of Chickmagalur, Coorg, Hassan, North Kanara and Shimoga would be in the plantations or forestry. In Bellary and Raichur it would be mining and quarrying. In Kolar district, mining would be the main activity for this category due to the existence of the Kolar Gold Mines.

The proportion in Category IV—Household Industry—is low being only 3.97% for the state. It is, however, 33.69%% in Coorg district, and the main activity is manufacture of wood and wooden products. In Bangalore district, the immigrants engaged in household industry constitute 8.68% of the proportion of the population of the district engaged in household industry. The main occupations include the production and rearing of livestock mainly for milk and animal power such as cows, goats, etc., and the rearing of silkworms and production of cocoons and raw silk. Cotton and silk weaving is also a prominent activity.

The proportion in Category V—manufacturing other than household industry, of immigrants to total population engaged in that category of industrial activity is 16.94%. The major proportions are in Bangalore district (26.56%), Bellary (22.84%), Coorg (59.37%), North Kanara (27.35%) and Shimoga (28.03%). In Bangalore District, the main activity is in the manufacture of textile goods, stone dressing, electrical goods manufacturing, and repair and in the air-craft factory and other central government factories. In Coorg, North Kanara and Shimoga districts, the manufacture of wood and wooden products is prevalent. In Shimoga district may of the immigrants are engaged in the iron works there.

In Category VI—construction—the proportion of immigrants to the population engaged in that activity is 36.07%. In Bangalore district the proportion is 31.62% and the main economic activity is building construction and maintenance. In Bellary district it is 54.89% and mainly engaged in the construction and maintenance of canals and bunds of the irrigation system in that district.

In 1971, out of the total population 99.89% are born within the country and the rest are from outside India. Nearly 96% of the total population in the state are born in the state. Of these, 68.74% are born at the place of enumeration, 20.54% are elsewhere in the district of enumeration and 6.66% are in other districts of the state. Migrants from outside the state form a very small proportion of 3.95% only and in that 3.70% is accounted for by migrants from the neighboring states of Tamil Nadu, Andhra Pradesh, Maharashtra, and Kerala. Tables given the distribution of population by place of birth as in 1971.

TABLE 19 : Born in India, within the state of enumeration

	Male	Female	Total
Born in the place of enumeration	11,495,864	8,644,514	20,140,378
Born elsewhere in the district of enumeration	2,065,842	3,953,558	6,019,410
Born in other districts of the state	832,717	1,118,741	1,951,458

It is observed that 93% of the immigrants are from the neighboring states of Tamil Nadu (29.81%), Andhra Pradesh (29.71%), Maharashtra (19.02%), and Kerala (15.61%). The proportion of migrants from other states is not significant except in the case of Rajasthan, which accounts for only 2.03%. Among the total immigrants, females exceed males in number from Andhra Pradesh, Maharashtra, and the union territories. The migration of females is obviously due to marriage and other socio-cultural factors. This also reflects the continued socio-cultural link of the northern districts of this state with the neighboring state of Andhra Pradesh and Maharashtra. In the case of other states, male migrants exceed female.

It can be seen from Table that Bangalore district has drawn the highest % (26.43%) of migrants from other states and union territories in India whereas the least is in Mandya district (1.23%). Next comes Belgaum district with 10.38% of the total migrants from other states. The other districts are having less than 10% of the migrants. Among males also Bangalore district with 30.57% comes 1st followed by Belgaum (7.79%) and South Kanara (7.19%), the least being from Bidar (1.42%). Among females Bangalore has absorbed the largest proportion with 22.53% followed by Belgaum (12.80%) and Kolar (7.55%). The least is in Mandya district with 1% of the total migrant population from outside the state.

About 62% of the total male migrants move to rural areas (53% from rural and 7% from urban to rural). On the other hand, 23% (13% from rural to urban, 10% from urban to urban) of the female migrants move to urban areas as against 38% (20% rural to urban, 18% urban to urban) for males. Here it is observed that the movement of males is more than that of females to urban areas where more job opportunities and educational facilities are available. Females move mainly in connection with family rather than for employment. If, we compare this movement within rural areas females move less from urban to rural than males (9.53% males and 7.36% females). The reason for this higher mobility among males may be seasonal migrations of males for contract jobs. Also male students may be moving to urban areas for education and on completion, returning home.

TABLE 20 :

Number of inter-state immigrants from other states and union territories and proportion they constitute in the total immigrant population of the Karnataka state, 1971

Birthplace State / Union Territory	Immigrants from other states and union territories				
	Persons		Male		Female
	Number	(%)	Number	(%)	Number
Total immigrants from other states	1,157,813	100.00	561,867	100.00	595,946
Andhra Pradesh	337,720	29.17	143,990	25.63	193,730
Assam	650	0.06	470	0.80	180
Bihar	2,845	0.25	2,140	0.38	705
Gujarat	8,460	0.74	4,845	0.86	3,615
Haryana	1,810	0.15	1,475	0.26	335
Himachal Pradesh	1,175	0.10	780	0.14	395
Jammu and Kashmir	655	0.06	500	0.08	155
Kerala	180,764	15.61	115,978	20.65	64,786
Madhya Pradesh	2,500	0.21	1,315	0.24	1,185
Maharashtra	220,160	19.02	73,475	13.08	146,685
Manipur	100	N	70	N	30
Meghalaya	10	N	5	N	5
Nagaland	55	N	25	N	30
Orissa	735	0.06	520	0.09	215

Punjab	4575	0.39	3.120	0.56	1.455
Rajasthan	23.465	2.03	15.350	2.74	8.115
Sikkim	10	N	10	N	--
Tamil Nadu	344.954	29.81	182.349	32.46	162.605
Tripura	40	N	30	N	10
Uttar Pradesh	8.910	0.76	6.065	1.08	2.845
West Bengal	4.115	0.36	2.500	0.45	1.615
Union Territories	14.105	1.22	6.855	122	7.250

Note: 'N'—Negligible

It is attempted here to analyze the trend and patterns

To analyze the trend and pattern of various types of migration, such as Intra-district, Inter-district, Inter-State, rural-rural, rural-urban, urban-urban, and urban-rural migration in Karnataka and to analyze the reason behind the migration.

TABLE 21:

Percentage distribution among districts of Karnataka state to total of immigrants from other states in India, 1971

State/ District	Person	Male	Female
Bangalore	26.43	30.57	22.53
Belgaum	10.38	7.79	12.80
Bellary	6.34	5.94	6.72
Bidar	3.38	1.42	5.25
Bijapur	3.50	2.73	4.23
Chikmagalur	2.65	3.23	2.10
Chitradurga	2.93	2.73	3.12
Coorg	3.82	5.04	2.68
Dharwad	2.53	2.87	2.20
Gulbarga	4.84	3.16	6.43
Hassan	1.68	2.13	1.26

Kolar	6.20	4.77	7.55
Mandya	1.23	1.46	1.00
Mysore	4.77	5.53	4.05
North Kanara	2.07	2.44	1.71
Raichur	4.13	4.53	3.76
Shimoga	3.49	4.18	2.84
South Kanara	6.33	7.19	5.50
Tumkur	3.30	2.29	4.27
Karnataka State	100.00	100.00	100.00

Source: Migration Tables of Karnataka 1971.

The Table 22 show the migration statistics which indicates that people of both Karnataka and India are becoming less mobile in nature. In the 2001 Census, 16.2 million persons out of total population of 52.8 million in Karnataka were enumerated at a place different from the place of birth and thus termed as migrants. This constitutes 30.62 percent of the total population of the state. In terms of absolute figures, number has increased from 9.1 million in 1971 to 11.7 million in 1981 to 13.3 million in 1991 and 16.2 million in 2001. It may, however, be noted that the percentage of migrants to total population has consistently declined from 31.26 percent in 1971 to 30.62 percent in 2001. In terms of total volume of migrants in India has increased from 166.8 million in 1971, 203.5 million in 1981, 229.8 million in 1991 and 307.1 million in 2001. The percentage of migrants to the total population of the country has also decreased from 30.42 percent in 1971to 29.86 percent in 2001.

Table 22: Distribution of population in percentage by migration status in Karnataka and India 1971-2001. (Birthplace criterion).

Year	1971			1981			1991			2001		
Karnataka												
	P %	M%	F%	P%	M%	F%	P%	M%	F%	P%	M%	F%
Migrants	31.26	23.22	39.66	31.49	22.36	40.96	29.55	20.01	39.50	30.62	26.65	40.95
New Migrants	68.74	74.72	60.34	68.51	77.54	59.04	70.45	79.99	60.50	69.38	79.35	59.05
Population (million)	29.29	14.97	14.33	37.13	18.52	18.21	44.97	22.95	22.02	52.85	26.89	25.95
India												
Migrants	36.42	18.93	47.79	30.60	17.82	44.28	27.41	14.63	41.20	29.86	16.99	43.66
New migrants	69.58	81.07	57.21	69.40	82.18	55.72	72.59	85.37	58.80	70.14	83.01	56.34
Population (million)	548.2	284.1	264.1	665.3	343.9	321.3	838.5	435.2	403.3	1028.6	532.2	496.4

Source: Census of India; Migration Tables of Karnataka and India from 1971 to 2001.

The sex wise differences are more prominent in Indian migration data. In 2001, 20.65 percent male and 40.95 percent female population were 1951enumerated outside their place of birth in Karnataka. The prevailing marriage custom in India of brides moving to place of groom after marriage terms most of female as migrants. As seen above that both Karnataka and Indian migration percentage has declined from 1971 to 2001. Whereas the percentage of non-migrant population has increased during the same period. The percentage of Karnataka migrants however in all these three censuses has been slightly higher than in India as a whole, the percentage of male migrants in Karnataka also is much higher than in India. However, it is striking to note that the percentage of female migrants is lower in Karnataka compared to India as a whole.

Distance and direction of migration flows:

The international migration data are presented in census reports at these levels viz., Intra-district, Inter-district, and Inter-State. Based on types of migration streams, data is presented in Table – 23 for 1971 to 2001. It indicates that distance plays an important role in migration process.

Table – 23. Percentage of Migrants at different distance level to total migrants in Karnataka and India in 1971 to 2001.

Year	1971			1981			1991			2001		
Karnataka												
Migration steam	PTM	Male%	F %	PTM	M %	F %	PTM	M %	F %	PTM	M %	F %
Intra District	65.72	39.43	69.37	61.88	54.30	66.24	61.55	54.24	65.41	58.90	50.96	63.27
Inter District	21.31	23.96	19.69	23.88	27.65	21.74	21.74	29.16	23.42	27.90	31.59	25.31
Inter State	12.64	16.16	10.49	13.95	17.68	11.43	12.46	12.44	10.74	13.02	17.35	10.76
International	0.23	0.34	0.19	0.29	0.47	0.28	6.38	0.31	0.21	0.27	0.50	0.15
INDIA												
Intra District	62.12	48.33	68.69	59.35	45.62	65.26	59.26	59.26	64.32	59.19	47.32	64.14
Inter District	21.10	24.64	19.41	25.01	28.89	23.34	25.72	25.72	24.43	25.02	29.41	24.02
Inter State	11.17	17.34	8.06	11.90	18.76	8.80	11.86	11.86	9.11	13.78	21.76	10.46
International	5.46	9.07	3.74	3.84	6.73	2.59	3.02	3.02	2.02	2.01	3.51	1.38

PTM-Percentage to total migrants.
Source: Census of India, 1971 to 2001, Karnataka part II-D migration Tables.

In both Karnataka and India migrants mainly move over short distances, they move within district. As distance increases proportion of migrants decreases. Regarding the sex differences in different streams, data indicates female dominance in short distance movement. Over decade, the sex ratio of migrants both in Karnataka and India shows improvement indicating more females in medium and long-distance migration also

Out of total migrants in Karnataka, intra-district migration dominates the three-distance streams. (See Table: 23) It has however been steadily decreasing from 65.72 percent in 1971 to 58.90 percent in 2001, whereas at the national level it declined from 62,12 percent to 59.19 percent. On the other hand, inter-district migration has increased from 21.31 percent in 1971 to 27.80 percent in 2001 in Karnataka and from 21.10 percent in 1971 to 25.02 percent in 2001 in India. The percentage of inter-state migration is also increased from 1971 to 2001 both in Karnataka and India. International migration at national level has decreased from 5.46 percent in 1971 to 2.01 percent in 2001 whereas in Karnataka it is increased from 0.23 percent to 0.27 percent. Inter-district, interstate and international male migration is higher than that of female migration in all the census years, whereas intra-district male migration is lower than female migration in both Karnataka and India. Inter-district and inter-state male and female migration has increased from 1971 to 2001, but intra-district male and female migration has decreased both in state and in the country. International male and female migration have increased in Karnataka whereas it has decreased in India.

Place of last residence

Based on the place of last residence, among the three migration streams, the proportion of intra-district migration has decreased whereas inter-district migration has increased from 1971 to 2001 for both in sexes. Volume of inter-state and international migration was more in 2001 than in 1971. Among the four directions of migration streams, rural to rural migration streams forms the most dominant streams in all the decades (see table -24). In 2001, the rural-to-rural streams of intra-district accounted for large percentage than inter-district and inter-state rural-rural migration, 62.08 percent compared to 36.75 and 28.37 percent respectively.

Table-24. Distribution of migrants by different streams of migration in Karnataka based on place of last residence and duration of residence to place of enumeration 1971 to 2001.

MOS	1971			1981			1991			2001		
&DOM	P%	M%	F%	P%	M%	F%	P%	M%	F%	P%	M%	F%
Total												
R-R	62.62	52.00	69.12	57.72	45.35	64.71	56.85	43.79	63.74	51.02	32.40	60.76
R-U	15.21	19.00	12.53	19.03	25.48	15.41	17.54	23.71	14.29	17.05	23.16	13.86
U-U	13.20	17.78	10.40	15.07	20.08	12.23	15.78	21.29	12.87	15.32	21.46	12.10
U-R	8.04	9.23	7.31	7.96	8.75	7.52	8.31	9.07	7.90	5.26	5.62	5.08
Unclassified	0.93	1.40	0.64	0.20	0.34	0.13	1.52	2.14	1.20	11.35	17.36	8.20

PATTERNS OF CHILD MIGRATION:

Children living and working away from home are some of the most vulnerable in society. Parents, family, friends, and home communities provide protections that reduce a child's susceptibility to abuse, exploitation, and the consequences of bad or poorly informed decisions. This chapter reviews the nascent literature on the prevalence, causes, and consequences of independent child labor migration. Measurement challenges have constrained progress on understanding this phenomenon. There is considerable scope for future research to transform how we think about issues related to the millions of children living and working away from their parents

Mobility of India's population has gradually been growing particularly since independence. In the context of a predominantly agricultural economy and a consistently fast-growing population the small and declining size of agricultural land holdings had been basic to the process of out-migration. The zeal to improve the standard of living has been another vital consideration which is vivid in increasing migration from small towns to big cities and the movement of landless agricultural laborer's (mostly belonging to scheduled castes) from rural areas to urban places. The proximity to urban-industrial concentrations and major construction sites was a strong pull factor. Migration can be a disturbing influence on educational attainment of children. Among all the migrant children in the cities, the plight of the children of migrant construction workers are the most miserable as they move from site to site in search of jobs.

This section has been prepared from the available data on child migrants and child migrant labor which is given in Indian Censuses of 1961 and 1971. It examines the amount and extent of state-wise child-migrants, child migrant labor in the cities of India. It analyses the nature of employment patterns of migrant children in the cities. The data for this is taken from D-IV Migration tables of 1961 census. Here the migrants are identified from the information of place of birth. This information fails to measure the intermediate and multiple movements. This error may not be very serious in the case of child migrants as many of them might not have made more than one movement. However, some of them, especially, those who made short distance movements might have identified as migrants just because of the custom prevalent in the country for a woman to return to her father's household for deliveries. This section also analyses data on child migrants in Bangalore city, Greater Bombay, Karnataka, for this purpose data regarding place of last residence in 1971 census are utilized. The information on place of last residence was collected in respect of every person irrespective of his place of birth if he had another place of normal residence before he came to the present place where he was enumerated. Therefore, migrants are all persons who have migrated at any time; thus, it includes return migrants. Besides, this information reflects direct movement between places.

Extent of child migrants in the cities of various states:

State-wise child migration rates in the cities according to the 1961 census are given in Table (Few of the town groups are also included in these data). Out of about 13.4 million child population in these cities about 3 million (22.8%) were recorded as migrants. The two states which had high child migration rates were Assam (54.5%) and Orissa (37.4%) and the two states with low rates were Jammu and Kashmir (8%) and Kerala (12.8%). In the case of total migrants, if Delhi is excluded, the states which recorded high rates of migration were Assam (61.2%) and Punjab (58.3%) and the low rates were in Jammu and Kashmir and Kerala. The extent of child migrants and the total migrants are positively associated. The rank correlation coefficient between these is +0.79 which is statistically significant at 1% level. Surprisingly it is found that the child migration rate is negatively associated with the sex ratio of the total stream. Thus, the data goes against the impression that the stream with more females have more children.

Corresponding to every 100 migrants aged 15 and above enumerated in the cities there were 22 child migrants. In Orissa and Assam, the ratio of child migrants was high, the lowest was in Maharashtra. If the ratio of young male migrants and female migrants to male aged 15 and above can be taken as a measure of family migration, around 1.1 dependent persons accompany or follow the male migrants aged 15 and above, in the cities of India. This measure indicates that family migration as low in the cities of Assam, Maharashtra, and West Bengal and high in all the South Indian cities, Cuttack city and in the cities of Rajasthan.

Child labor in the cities of various states:

Child labor is a social evil which cannot be easily abolished. If poverty exists it will persist in some form or another. Another reason for child labor is that is attractive to employers because children work for lower wages than adults and because they do not have statutory rights and privileges. At the time of industrial revolution, there had been widespread exploitation of child labor in the western countries. In India, child labor is banned in many of the organized sectors. Due to these legal restrictions, many children due to practical necessity of work are forced to work in the unorganized sector, where working conditions are atrocious. They are often exploited. Out of 3 million child migrants in these cities, about 98 thousand (3.2%) were workers. Sex-wise work participation ratio was 4.8% for males and 1.4% of females. Between the states there are great variations. The work participation ratio among male children was observed in Jammu and Kashmir (8.7%) and lowest in Gujarat (2.4%). Among females the highest work participation ratio was in Kerala (7.5%) and lowest in Orissa (0.1%). Kerala is the only state where WPR of girls was greater than boys. It is surprising that the highest work participation ratio among young migrant girls was in the same state where child labor is the lowest and the educational level of women is the highest. In many socio-demographic characteristics Kerala is different from rest of India. Work participation ratio of child migrants in this state is also different from the rest. Poor families in Kerala do not feel relevant to send boys as well as girls for work away from their home. Some of the difference in the work participation ratio of children by state could be due to the difference in the age composition within the age group 0-14. Standardization is not possible as the age composition is not known.

TABLE 23: State-wise data regarding migration rate among total population, sex ratio of total migrants, young migrants as percentage of total aged 15 and above, ratio of young migrants and female migrants aged 15 and above t total male migrants aged 15 and above, WPR among young migrant, young migrant workers as percentage of young workers to the cities of various states, 1961

States / Central Territories	Migration Rate		Sex ratio of migrant's females/ males	Young migrants. Total migrants aged 15 and above (%)	Young male migrants and total female migrants (male migrants age 15+)	WPR of young migrants		Young migrant workers as percentage of young workers	
	Total Population	Children				M	F	M	F
Andhra Pradesh (11)*	36.8	21.1	1009	29.4	1.5	6.9	3.0	28.3	39.7
Assam (1)	61.2	54.5	396	38.2	0.7	4.8	0.7	88.7	54.7
Bihar (7)	43.9	21.0	795	23.0	1.2	7.4	1.4	44.8	32.3
Gujarat (6)	44.3	21.4	825	23.7	1.2	2.4	0.5	36.6	26.2
Jammu and Kashmir (2)	19.8	8.0	938	20.6	1.3	8.7	0.2	13.7	2.5
Kerala (5)	30.0	12.8	975	20.3	1.4	6.5	7.5	46.3	52.4
Madhya Pradesh (8)	48.7	22.0	814	21.5	1.2	3.5	1.8	35.4	40.1
Tamil Nadu (9)	36.7	16.6	907	20.1	1.3	5.4	2.5	28.0	31.3
Maharashtra (12)	58.3	27.1	652	19.1	0.9	5.4	2.0	62.0	47.3
Karnataka (6)	38.9	18.8	901	24.0	1.3	7.2	2.9	30.0	31.7
Orissa (1)	37.2	37.4	755	51.5	1.6	5.1	0.1	46.9	3.9
Punjab (5)	58.3	24.3	789	19.7	1.1	6.1	0.4	63.6	41.8
Rajasthan (6)	36.5	20.4	899	29.9	1.4	3.6	0.8	26.8	28.3

Uttar Pradesh (17)	37.8	17.6	831	23.0	1.1	5.4	0.8	26.6	35.2
West Bengal (12)	54.6	30.5	495	21.6	0.8	3.0	0.3	43.3	47.1
D.M.C. and New Delhi (2)	64.8	32.5	756	25.0	1.2	3.9	0.5	67.3	59.5
ALL INDIA (109)	46.9	22.8	735	22.3	1.1	4.8	1.4	38.5	38.7

Source:

1. Census of India, 1961, Vol. I, Part II-C (iii), India, Migration Tables (1)-IV.

2. Census of India, 1961, Vol. I, Part II-B (i), India, General Economic Tables (B-II).

* The figures inside the brackets are the number of cities.

In the cities of India, nearly 79% of the child workers were boys. In Orissa and Jammu and Kashmir almost all the workers were boys. Kerala is the only state where migrant's female workers outnumbered male workers. It may be noted that in the cities of Kerala the participation rate of non-migrant female children was also slightly higher than the rate of male children. This phenomenon observed in Kerala may be due to the limited type of jobs available for children.

Nearly 39% of the child workers in the cities were migrants. In Assam 82% of the children's workers were migrants while the percentage of Jammu and Kashmir was only 13%. If the workers among male children are only considered it has been observed that 89% of the workers in Assam, 76% in Delhi and 64% in Punjab were migrants. It has been further observed that the proportion of migrants among the child labor is directly associated with the child migration rate. The rank correlation between the child migration rate and the proportion of migrants a month the child workers is 0.77 which is statistically significant at 1% level. In the case of males, it is observed that in the cities of Kerala, Bihar, Punjab, Delhi, Maharashtra and Tamil Nadu, the ranks of child migration rate exceeded the ranks of migrants among child labor. Maximum difference is registered for Kerala. This indicates that compared to other cities to the cities of these states male children would be migrating for employments. In these cities WPR of male children were also high. Delhi was an exception. The case of Jammu and Kashmir was peculiar because here both the child migration rate as well as the migrants among child labor were the lowest but the WPR of migrant male children was the highest. In Jammu and Kashmir, the WPR of non-migrant male children was also the highest. This could be due to the very low literacy level of the people in this state.

Occupational composition of working migrant children in the cities:

Distribution of child workers in each of the states by occupational divisions are given in Table 3.2 and Table 3.3. Out of 77 thousand child migrant workers about 18 thousand were working in Maharashtra. Nearly 64% of the working males were working in Maharashtra, Uttar Pradesh, West Bengal, Andhra Pradesh, and Delhi. More than 9 in 10 of migrant males were occupied in three occupational divisions, namely, 'Craftsmen and Laborer's (43.5%), 'Services' (36.9%) and 'Sales' (10.9%). The type of work done by male children in the cities of different states is shown in Table. In Orissa (Cuttack city) about 53% of the migrant boys were employed in 'Sales' while in Kerala only 3.9% were engaged in this division. In contrast 82% of the child workers in cities of Kerala were employed in 'services.

Maximum differentials with respect to occupational distribution, from the all-India pattern is observed for states Kerala and Orissa which is revealed by the summary measure of the coefficient of dissimilarity (46.7 and 43.0, respectively). The maximum measure of co-efficient of dissimilarity is observed for Punjab. Out of total 75 occupational groups, only 12 were relevant for migrant male children. Nearly 60% of the workers were employed in 5 occupational divisions, namely (1) housekeepers; (2) laborer's not elsewhere classified (13.7%); (3) Waiters, bartenders, and related workers (7.3%); (4) Salesmen, shop assistants and related worker (7.1%); (5) Spinners, weavers, knitters, dyers and related workers, (6.5%). Thus, good number of these boys were employed by the affluent families and small hotels. Cuttack is the only city which did not employ migrant boys as domestic help and in small hotels while in cities of Kerala 77% of the working boys were employed in this group. More than half of the working boys in Cuttack city were employed as 'Salesmen shop assistant and related workers. When a search is made to find out the probable reasons for this difference, it has been observed that the occupational distribution of migrants in the cities of Kerala were different from that in Cuttack city. In cities of Kerala nearly 12% of the migrants were employed in professional occupations against 3% in Cuttack city. Thus, the migrants in cities of Kerala could afford to have domestic help. Besides, WPR among migrant females in Kerala were almost double that in Cuttack city. Nearly 10% of the workers in Cuttack city were employed in household industry, while in the cities of Kerala only 3.4% were thus employed. Majority of child migrants in Cuttack city could get jobs in the sales of household manufactured goods while those in Kerala could get employed in households as domestic help or in small hotels or restaurants.

TABLE 24: Percentage distribution of migrant working children in the cities by occupational divisions and state of enumeration, 1961

Occupational Divisions	Males															
	Andhra Pradesh	Assam	Bihar	Guj arat	Jammu and Kash mir	Karn ataka	Kerala	Madhya Pradesh	Maha rashtra	Ori ssa	Pun jab	Rajas than	Tamil Nadu	Uttar Pra desh	West Ben gal	Delhi
Cultivators	0.7	-	0.7	0.2	0.2	3.9	0.1	1.5	0.2	-	0.8	0.4	0.1	0.3	0.1	0.3
Agricultural Laborer's	1.8	-	0.6	0.4	0.2	2.9	-	1.0	0.8	-	0.8	0.7	0.4	0.6	0.1	0.2
Professional	0.8	-	0.7	0.5	-	1.3	0.4	0.5	0.9	1.3	0.4	2.6	0.3	3.2	1.1	0.8
Administrative	0.2	-	0.3	0.5	-	0.2	0.1	0.1	0.7	-	0.7	2.4	0.4	1.0	0.2	1.1
Clerical	3.3	0.5	1.0	1.7	1.5	2.5	0.5	0.8	1.4	1.3	0.5	3.1	1.9	3.5	1.9	1.0
Sales	9.3	5.0	6.4	12.3	5.6	8.0	3.9	10.9	12.2	53.0	10.1	12.8	15.6	10.0	14.9	5.2
Farmers	4.7	-	3.0	4.2	1.8	3.9	0.4	3.8	1.6	-	1.3	1.7	2.4	1.6	0.7	0.8
Miners	0.3	-	-	-	-	0.1	-	0.7	0.1	-	-	0.3	-	-	-	0.5
Transport	1.0	1.2	0.2	2.6	0.2	0.6	2.2	0.5	0.6	-	0.5	2.5	0.8	1.0	0.4	0.5
Craftsmen and Laborer's	58.7	64.8	23.0	35.9	22.5	49.8	10.1	57.5	36.2	44.4	45.9	53.1	52.8	54.1	36.0	38.0
Services	19.2	28.3	62.6	41.7	68.0	26.2	82.2	22.6	45.1	-	39.0	19.1	25.2	23.4	43.1	51.4
Unclassified	-	0.2	1.5	-	-	0.6	0.1	0.1	0.2	-	-	1.3	0.1	1.3	1.5	0.2
Total	100.0	100.0	100.0	100.0	100.0	100.0	100.0	100.0	100.0	100.0	100.0	100.0	100.0	100.0	100.0	100.0
No. of Cases	6855	400	4137	2382	594	5270	1137	2904	18045	525	3369	1662	5774	10473	7712	6141
Co-efficient of dissimilarity	20.52	21.74	27.65	10.00	31.11	14.27	46.74	17.34	9.56	43.07	4.38	18.66	14.23	15.59	11.12	15.42

Source: Census of India, 1961, Vol. I, Part III-C (iii), India, Migration Table (D-IV).

TABLE 25:

Percentage distribution of migrant working children in the cities by occupational divisions and state of enumeration, 1961

Occupational Divisions	Females															
	Andhra Pradesh	Assam	Bihar	Gujrat	Jammu and Kasmir	Karnataka	Kerala	Madhya Pradesh	Maharashtra	Orissa	Punjab	Rajasthan	Tamil Nadu	Uttar Pradesh	West Bengal	Delhi
Cultivators	1.5	-	2.1	2.9	-	8.8	-	4.1	0.9	-	-	2.9	0.2	2.0	-	2.9
Agricultural Laborer's	4.8	-	3.9	1.2	-	2.3	0.1	1.5	2.8	-	2.0	4.1	0.9	0.8	0.2	3.2
Professional	0.9	-	1.8	2.0	9.1	0.5	0.2	0.4	2.0	-	1.5	6.1	0.7	7.6	7.1	1.9
Administrative	0.1	-	0.1	-	-	-	-	-	0.2	-	1.0	0.7	0.1	-	-	-
Clerical	0.3	-	0.5	0.2	-	0.5	-	0.1	0.4	-	-	0.9	0.1	0.4	0.4	-
Sales	3.0	-	2.6	2.2	-	1.1	-	1.2	2.2	100.00	3.0	2.5	1.3	2.4	3.5	3.2
Farmers	0.8	3.4	1.7	9.3	-	3.1	-	2.0	0.5	-	2.4	5.4	0.7	4.6	0.4	1.2
Miners	0.9	-	-	0.7	-	0.2	-	1.1	0.1	-	-	0.9	-	-	-	2.6
Transport	-	-	-	2.5	-	-	-	0.1	0.1	-	-	0.2	0.1	-	-	-
Craftsmen and Laborer's	48.2	6.8	41.4	49.5	18.2	48.3	2.8	72.7	43.9	-	54.2	55.3	37.8	56.0	35.1	37.7
Services	39.4	89.8	45.8	29.5	72.7	34.8	96.9	16.8	46.9	-	35.9	21.0	58.1	25.0	51.7	46.4
Unclassified	0.1		0.1	-	-	0.4	-	-	-	-	-	-	-	1.2	1.6	0.9
Total	100.0	100.0	100.0	100.0	100.0	100.0	100.0	100.0	100.0	100.0	100.0	100.0	100.0	100.0	100.0	100.0
No. of Cases	*3431	(59)	725	410	11	2175	1307	1296	5873	7	203	443	2523	1307	510	758
Co-efficient of dissimilarity	7.94	46.85*	3.38	16.95	35.12*	12.90	52.08	32.82	2.86	97.98*	12.85	21.08	13.31	22.25	15.07	7.21

Source: Census of India, 1961, Vol. I, Part III-C (iii), India, Migration Table (D-IV).

Out of 21 thousand migrants working girls 28% were working in Maharashtra and 16% were working in Andhra Pradesh. If we include Tamil Nadu and Karnataka also in these four states, 2/3rds of the girls were working. In the case of female workers, nearly 9 out of 10 were employed in the two occupational divisions (1) 'services' (44.9%) and (2) 'Craftsmen and laborer's (44.1%). About 2/3rds of the working girls were employed in the 3 occupational categories: (1) housekeepers, cooks, maids, and related workers (40.6%); (2) 'Laborer's not elsewhere classified' (14.6%); and (3) 'Spinners, weavers, knitters, dyers and related workers' (11.3%). Thus, among girls at least 4 in 10 were employed by the affluent families. In Kerala almost all the migrant female workers were working as housekeepers, cooks, maids and related workers. The lowest proportion in this category was observed in Uttar Pradesh.

The literacy level of migrant workers in Gujarat and Punjab were higher than the rest. The lowest literacy level was observed for the migrant workers in Jammu and Kashmir and Orissa (Table). In all the cities of the states, the literacy level of young migrant workers was lower than the young migrants. The magnitude of the difference in the literacy level of the migrants and that of the workers could have been measured in a better way, if the literacy level of persons aged 5-15 years were compared. Nevertheless, this table indicates that the child migrant workers had a lower literacy than the child migrants. Overall, about 11% of the male workers and nearly 5% of the female workers had an educational level of primary and above. Migrant working children were from families of lower socio-economic status.

TABLE 26:

Percentage primary and above among young migrants and young migrant workers in the cities of each of the states in India.

States of Enumeration	Young migrants		Young migrant workers
	Males	Females	Males
Andhra Pradesh	25.4	19.4	13.0
Assam	32.9	18.7	10.5
Bihar	20.5	13.0	2.8
Gujarat	37.1	34.3	25.3
Jammu and Kashmir	10.4	7.6	0.8
Karnataka	24.2	19.5	9.6
Kerala	22.9	21.4	10.6
Madhya Pradesh	11.0	8.9	6.3
Maharashtra	23.8	19.7	14.8
Orissa	22.3	14.8	1.1
Punjab	30.5	27.6	23.2
Rajasthan	6.9	4.4	1.1
Tamil Nadu	29.1	24.4	18.4
Uttar Pradesh	21.3	12.9	6.6
West Bengal	19.7	16.9	6.0
Delhi	18.3	17.7	8.3
All India	22.6	18.4	11.2

Child migrants and child labor in cities:

According to 1961 census in Greater Bombay, out of 400,754 child migrants, 16,643 (4.2%) were working and 78% of these workers were males. According to 1961 census in Bangalore city, out of 83,869 child migrants, 4,604 (5.49%) were working and 74% of these workers were males. Data regarding child migrant workers are not directly available in 1971 census. Only the combined figure of migrant workers aged 0-15 and 60 and above is available. The migrant workers aged 60 and above can be estimated form the total workers aged 60 and above assuming that the ratio of work participation rate of migrants to total workers by age group is same in 1961 and 1971. The estimated child workers in Bangalore city are 45,02 (4.96%). According to this estimate the child migrant labor is nearly 74% of the child labor in Bangalore city. The slight decline observed in WPR in Bangalore city in 1971 could be due to the change in the concept of worker at the two censuses. Students doing secondary work being excluded in 1971 census could be very high.

It has been found that the extent of child migrants is positively associated with the extent of total migrants in the cities of India. Nearly 23% of the children in the cities were recorded as migrants. Corresponding to every hundred migrants aged 15 and above enumerated in the cities of India there were 22 child migrants. Between the states the extend of child migration to the cities varied. The highest child migration rate was in Assam (Gulati city 55%) and lowest was in Jammu and Kashmir (8%). Workers constituted 3.2% of the child migrants in the cities. Nearly 8 in 10 of the migrant child workers were males. Only in the cities of Kerala, female migrant child workers out-numbered male workers and the highest work participation among female children was also in Kerala.

Nearly 39% of the child workers in the cities were migrants. It ranged from 8.2% in Assam to 13% in Jammu and Kashmir. The general observation was that wherever the total migration was high the proportion of migrant child labor was also high. Migrant children were employed only in certain type of jobs mainly because of their age, training, suitability and because child labor is cheap. More than 9 in 10 migrant male children were occupied in 4 occupational divisions—namely ‘Craftsmen and laborer’s (43.5%), services (36.9%), and sales (10.9%). Nearly 25% of male children and 41% of female children were employed in the single occupational category ‘housekeepers, cooks, maids and related workers. Therefore, the maximum proportion of migrant children were employed by the affluent families and small hotels or restaurants. The distribution of these young migrant workers by occupational categories varied between states. Higher incidence of migrant child labor may be due to various reasons like the extent of general migration, availability of jobs, socio-economic level of the population of the sending areas, etc. The cause of child labor and the conditions under which they work are not known from census data. Economic compulsion is stated as the major reason for the children to join the labor force by some of the special studies.2 The type of work in which they are engaged involves long hours of respective work without proper holidays and the remuneration especially as domestic help or in hotels and restaurants are very low. Type of migrations of children in states show that majority of rural children made short distance migrations, while migrant children in the urban areas mostly made long distance migrations. The type of migration made by children was very much also with that of the orders. Even though the child migration was mostly due to sequential reasons, extent of child migration and especially the working migrants depends on various other factors. This requires a special study.

Chapter IV

THE RURAL URBAN INTERNAL MIGRATION
Its Socio-Economic Correlates

Studies starting from Revenstein (1885 and 1889) have tried to account for the migration differences through certain chosen variables. Zipf (1946) proposed that number of migrants is directly proportional to distance. For Stouffer (1940), it is availability of opportunities at destination which account for migration. Prior migration is considered to be important by Greenwood (1969). Combining Zipf and Greenwood's propositions and taking into account both distance and previous migration, Trever and Mcleod (1973) were successful in predicting inter-state migration in U.S.A. Significant correlations have also been found between a current and previous migration in India (Singh and Yadav 1974). Stouffer's availability of opportunities is in a way related to prior migration for it is mostly through previous migrants that this reaches potential migrant, and Zipf's geographic distance is countered by psychological (Burford 1962) and social distance depending on presence or absence of Kin at places of destination. A comprehensive econometric model includes all these variables to predict the volume of migration.

$$Mij = f(Yij : UiUj; ZiZj; Dij, Cij)$$

Where, I = Place of origin, and j = Place of destination.
Mij = Variable explaining migration.
Y = Income levels.
U = Unemployment rates.
Z = Degree of Urbanization.
Dij = Distance between place of origin and place of destination.
Cij = Friends and relatives in place of destination (World Bank Staff Working Paper 1975).

Density of population, agricultural productivity is correlated with migration, positively in the case of former and negatively in case of latter (Dasgupta and Laishley 1975). A tendency for better educated to be more mobile is often reported (Thomas 1938, Caldwell 1969). When certain geographic/administrative units are considered, how far the differential rate of migration are explained by these variables? The basic difficulty in this issue is the unit of consideration. If the unit is too small or too large the variable explains everything or nothing, respectively. The districts in Karnataka are taken as units for comparison here and 1960-61 and 1970-71 data from published reports are analyzed.

How far the variables viz. (1) density of population; (2) percentage of literates; (3) births per 100 in the year 1960 and 1970; (4) percentage of households in agricultural occupation; (5) percentage of area sown twice to net area sown; (6) food-grain production per acre in kg.; (7) percentage of populations dependent on agricultural wages for livelihood, are related to the proportion of non-migrants namely: rural-rural, rural-urban, urban-rural and urban-urban is bested. According to 1961 census, 22.33%t (11.67 per cent males; 10.66% females) of Karnataka population is urban as against to 24.31% (12.71% males; 11.60% females) of Karnataka in 1971 census is urban. Similarly, 77.67% (39.38% males; 38.29% females) is rural in 1961; as against to that of 1971 census 75.69% (38.39% males; 37.30% females) is rural. As could be seen from Table 4.1, 69-75% of rural and 60.97% of urban population are born and enumerated in the same place or 'locally born' in 1961 census. Whereas in 1971, 70.31% of rural and 63.85% of urban population are 'locally born'.

The data would indicate that quite a large proportion of the total population is not mobile both in 1961 and 1971 census. It is interesting to notice that the degree of migration is less among males than among females. Of the males in the total population, during 1961 census, 76.22% are enumerated in their place of birth as against 59.00% of females. During 1971 census of the males in the total population,

76.78% are enumerated in their place of birth as against 60.34% of females. There is generally greater migration among females. In 1961 census in the rural areas, 69.75% of the population is at the place of their birth; 80.20% of the rural males and 59.01% of the rural females have been enumerated at their place of birth. In the urban areas, 60.97% of the population, or 62.97% of the urban males and 58.92% of the urban females have been enumerated in their place of birth. Whereas in 1971 census in the rural areas, 70.31% of the population is at the place of their birth; 80.55% of the rural males and 59.76% of the rural females have been enumerated at their place of birth. In the urban areas, 63.85% of the population, or 65.37% of the urban males and 62.18% of the urban females have been enumerated in their place of birth. There is a greater proportion of migration in the urban areas. The proportion of females who remain in their places of birth in the rural and urban areas are almost equal in 1961, while the proportion of rural males who have not moved out of their place of birth is much higher than that of urban males in both the census. The greater degree of migration among females is due to the custom of the bride moving to the place where her husband lives, or in other words has been explained in terms of 'marriage' and 'associational' migration. Marriage results in a large number of female moving out of their place of birth.

Table 26:Percentage of population born in place of enumeration 1961-1971

	1961			1971	
	Persons	Male	Females	Persons	Male
Total	97.79	76.22	59.00	68.74	76.78
Rural	69.75	80.20	59.01	70.31	80.55
Urban	60.97	62.79	58.98	63.85	65.37

TABLE 27:

Migration in Karnataka (Percentages), 1961-71

Type of Migration	1961(Census)				1971(Census)		
	Migrated				Migrated to		
	Rural		Urban		Rural		Urban
	Male	Female	Male	Female	Male	Female	Male
Non-immigrant to:							
Rural	31.58	22.60	-	-	30.93	22.29	-
Urban	-	-	7.33	6.28	-	-	8.31
Intra-district Migrants:							
Rural	4.95	11.67	1.23	1.46	4.74	10.59	1.33
Urban	0.35	0.56	0.51	0.58	0.51	0.90	0.46
Inter-district Migrant:							
Rural	1.23	1.91	0.68	0.62	1.04	1.94	0.72
Urban	0.20	0.25	0.64	0.66	0.29	0.40	0.78
Inter-state Migrants:							
Rural	0.81	1.04	0.66	0.52	0.59	0.89	0.47
Urban	0.14	0.13	0.56	0.49	0.23	0.22	0.60

Total population: 23,586,772 (1961 census) (100%);
29,299,014 (1971 census) (100%)

Note: Population categorized by census as unclassifiable belonging to neither urban nor rural categories are not included in the table, but the total population figures include them also.

TABLE 28:

Intra-state migration in Karnataka (Percentages), 1961-71

Type of Migration	1961 (Census)				1971(Census)		
	Migrated				Migrated to		
	Rural		Urban		Rural		Urban
	Male	Female	Male	Female	Male	Female	Male
Intra-district Migrants:							
Rural	17.99	42.37	4.48	5.30	17.42	38.94	4.88
Urban	1.28	2.05	1.85	2.09	1.87	3.29	1.71
Inter-district Migrant:							
Rural	4.46	6.92	2.48	2.25	3.83	7.15	2.65
Urban	0.72	0.90	2.32	2.40	1.08	1.45	2.86

Total population: 6,494,543 (100%) (1961 census)
7,970,868 (100%) (1971 census)

Source:

1. Table D-II, Census of India, 1961, Vol. XI, Mysore, Part-II-C (ii), Migration Tables.

2. Table D-I, Census of India, 1971, Series-14, Mysore, Part-II-D, Migration Tables.

Note: Population categorized by census as unclassifiable belonging to neither urban nor rural categories are not included in the table, but the total population figure includes them also.

The proportion of immobility or locally born population as may be seen from Table 4.2 and 4.3 both for 1961 and 1971 census generally accounts for a major portion of the total, rural and urban population in the state. The rural areas in general have higher proportion of immobile population than in urban areas which mainly is due to the agro-based occupational structure. Exceptional to this rule being Bidar district, where proportions of these locally born in urban areas (74.39%) (which incidentally is the highest proportion among the districts) is slightly higher than that in rural areas (73.77%). As against to that in 1961 census also Bidar district, where proportions of those locally born in urban areas (74.82%) (which incidentally is the highest proportion among the districts) is slightly higher than that in rural areas (72.72%). Coorg district has the lowest proportion of locally born persons in all the areas and in fact urban population has shown a higher mobility with its only 42.61% of locally born persons.

The sex ratio of locally born persons (i.e., 963. 954 and 1,004 females per 1,000 males in total, rural and urban areas, respectively in 1961 census, in South Kanara district. Similarly in Tumkur district is the lowest among the districts with 675, 666 and 783 in total, among the districts both in 1961 and 1971 census with 666,637 and 899 in total, rural and urban areas, respectively. Even in 1971 census South Kanara districts stands 1st in sex-ratio with 953, 946 and 978 in total, rural and urban areas, respectively.

The total percentage of immigrants in the state including those born outside India and those who are unclassifiable would be 4.67% in 1961 and 4.04% in 1971 census. It will be noticed from the data that the percentage of immigrants to the total population is particularly high in the districts of Bangalore, Bellary, Coorg, Kolar and Shimoga. The immigration into Bangalore Metropolitan area and is largely due to the industrial complex that exists in this area. The district of Bellary attracts a large element of immigrations mainly into the rural areas due to the irrigation potentialities there. The districts of Coorg and Shimoga attract immigrants due to the vast plantations that require labor in these two districts. Kolar district has a large element of immigration due to the existence of Kolar Gold Mines in that district. However, the proportion of immigrants to the total population is not considerable excepting in the districts of Bangalore and Coorg. By and large, therefore, immigration, as such, does not constitute a major determinant in the size of the population of the districts in the state.

Of the migrants within the district, 29.80% are males and 70.20% are females, who have migrated from one rural area to another rural area within the same district in 1961. Whereas in 1971 census 30.91% are males and 69.09% are females. The high proportion of females support the general conclusion made earlier that the migration is more social than economic and mainly due to marriage. The proportion of women increases with the duration. The proportions between males and females are approximately equal only in the one year and less category. This preponderance of females in all the durations in again an indication of the influence of economic factors on migration within the same district is not prominent. The seasonal migration caused by agricultural operations would not be fully reflected in the data as the enumeration in March would only catch the tail end of the 'Rabi' season. In those districts where the 'Rabi' crop is important, short duration migration is prominent. These are Belgaum, Bajaur, Dharwad and Gulbarga mainly.

Rural to urban migration within the same district due to marriage is very much less prominent in the rural to urban migration pattern. The main motivation for migration from the rural areas to the urban is economic. Bangalore district has the highest number of such migrants as is to be expected since the industrialization in and around Bangalore city is a strong influence. The districts of Dharwad, Bajaur, South Kanara, Belgaum, and Mysore have also large number of such migrants. Table 4.2 gives the detailed distributions of migrants and non-migrant populations for both the sexes. Largest proportion of Karnataka population is constituted of non-migrant rural population. The inter-district and inter-state immigrants constitute higher proportion in rural-to-rural migration in both the above-mentioned categories. The intra-district rural to rural female migrants are second largest. This may be due to the marital migration and patrilocal residence. This percentage rapidly falls in inter-district migration. When migrants alone are considered (Table 4.3) intra-district rural-rural migration is most frequent (C.F. Kshirasagar 1973, NSS, 1960, Zachariah 1964, Vidyasagar 1978). The difference between males and females is largest in rural-rural migration. In all other types of migrations, the gap closes in and in only inter-district rural-urban migration males constitute greater percentage than females. Another important feature is that rural-rural migration is most frequent in both inter- and intra-district migration. In inter-state immigration it is least frequent.

The following statement brings out movement from rural to rural, rural to urban, urban to rural, and urban to urban areas in 1971 census.

TABLE 29:

Inter-state migration to Karnataka 1971

Place of last residence	Males enumerated in			Females enumerated in	
	Rural	Urban	Total	Rural	Urban
Rural	1,817,930 (52,74%)	685,280 (19.88%)	2,503,210 (72,62%)	3,952,070 (72.62%)	715,200 (12.61%)
Urban	322,330 (9.35%)	621,395 (19.03%)	943,725 (27.38%)	418,020 (7.36%)	595,055 (10.47%)
Total	(62.09%)	(37.91%)	(100.00%)	(76.92%)	(23.08%)

Note:

(i) The % to total migrants of each sex is given within brackets

(ii) Figures of unclassifiable last place of residence are excluded.

About 62% of the total male migrants move to rural areas (53% from rural to rural and 9% from urban to rural) whereas this % goes up to 77% for females (70% from rural to rural and 7% from urban to rural). On the other hand, 23% (13% from rural to urban, 10% from urban to urban) of the female migrants move to urban areas as against 38% (20% rural to urban, 18% urban to urban) for males. Here, it is observed that the movement of males is more than that of females to urban areas where more job opportunities and educational facilities are available. Females move mainly in a connection with family and other social reasons rather than for employment. If we compare this movement within rural areas females move less from urban to rural than males (9.35% males and 7.36% females). The reason for this bigger mobility among males may be seasonal migrations of males for contract jobs. Also, male students may be moving to urban areas for education and on completion, returning home. Table 30 gives the sex ratio in migrant population by types of movement during 1971 census.

TABLE 30:Number of females per thousand males, 1971

Last Residence	Place of enumeration	
	Rural	Urban
Rural	2,174	1,045
Urban	1,297	958
Total	2,042	1,004

Note: Figures pertaining to unclassifiable place of last residence not included.

Marriage migration forms an important of total migration and this is largely responsible for the imbalances in the sex ratio of migrant population. The sex ratio among migrants as may be seen from Table 4.5 is 1,648 which is highly in favor of females. The sex ratio in different types of movements, namely, rural to rural (2,174), urban to rural (1,279) and rural to urban (1,045) are also significantly higher in favor of females. In the urban to urban (958) movement alone we see that the sex ratio is in favor of males. The high sex ratio in the rural-to-rural movement in favor of females indicates the intensity of marriage migration of females between rural to rural areas which is not uncommon in the background that out population is predominantly rural. The different standards of life other social factors in rural and urban areas may act as a deterrent for the marriages taking place between these two areas thus resulting in relatively lesser degree movement. Further the lesser movement of males from urban to rural areas and higher mobility of males seasonal and urban to urban areas in search of better employment, for education, etc., are some of the reasons attributable for the varying sex ratios among migrants of different types.

Correlates of migration

Table 31 gives the inter-correlation matrix of these variables. Only male migration is considered because the female marital migration would distort the correlations. The zero order correlations with % of non-migrants in district as weak on variables; % or agricultural laborer's; density per square mile; slightly high but still weak on birth rate; moderate on gross food grain production per acre; and considerably high on % of literates and persons in primary sector occupations. All except density and people in primary sector occupation are negatively correlated. That is, the more the literacy, lesser will be sedentary population in a district and people in agricultural occupations, and higher will be the intra-district rural-urban and urban-rural migrations. The more the people involved in primary sector occupations in a district the lesser will be the urban-to-urban migration in it. More the gross production of food grains in a district, lesser will be people dependent on agricultural wages, more will be urban to rural migrants and lesser will be the sedentary population. As the urban-rural migration in a district increases the sedentary population in a district decreases. Because of the moderately high correlation (about 0.5) of this with other types of migration this can be used as a maker among the migration variables used here. When the other variables are controlled, density per square mile increases in its explanatory power (as increase in partial R-square in Table 4.7), and that of literacy and people in agricultural occupations, decreases. The inter-correlations between migration variables are considerably high.

TABLE 31:

Inter-correlation matrix between migration and six other selected variables

Variables										
1	2	3	4	5	6	7	8	9	10	11
-	-0.358	-0.171	-0.481	-0.211	0.171	-0.262	-0.262	0.642	-0.459	-0.111
		0.506	0.643	-0.096	-0.213	0.470	0.739	-0.253	0.229	0.685
			0.412	0.541	0.394	0.582	0.594	-0.369	-0.112	0.393
				0.412	-0.324	0.577	0.755	-0.265	0.392	0.091
					0.454	0.444	0.256	-0.570	-0.145	-0.063
						0.217	-0.007	-0.122	-0.596	0.313
							0.513	-0.592	0.215	0.306
								-0.120	0.163	0.374
									-0.123	-0.279
										-0.276

Note: Names of the variables:

1. Percentage of non-migrants in the district

2. Percentage of intra-district rural to rural migration in the total population

3. Percentage of intra-district rural to urban migration in the total population

4. Percentage of intra-district urban to rural migration in the total population

5. Percentage of intra-district urban to urban migration in the total population

6. Density of population per square mile

7. Percentage of literates in the total population

8. Births per 1,000 people in 1960 and 1970

9. Percentage of people in agricultural occupation

10. Per capita food grain production per acre (in Kg.)

11. Area sown twice to the total area cropped

12. Percentage of household dependent on agricultural wages.

Sources:

1-5 Table D-II, Census of India, 1961, Vol. XI, Mysore, Part II-C (ii), Migration Tables

6. Statement II-32, Census of India, 1961, Vol. XI, Mysore, Part I (A), General Report

7. Statement VII-I, Census of India, 1961, Vol. XI, Mysore, Part I (A), General Report

8. Table-8.4, Number of live births in 1960, VIII, Public Health and Vital Statistics, Statistical Abstract of Mysore, 1960-61, Department of Statistics, Government of Mysore (1963)

9. Statements X-39, Census of India, 1961, Vol. XI, Mysore, Part I (A), General Report

10. Statements X-64, Census of India, 1961, Vol. XI, Mysore, Part I (A), General Report

11. Statements X-58, Census of India, 1961, Vol. XI, Mysore, Part I (A), General Report

12. Statements X-63, Census of India, 1961, Vol. XI, Mysore, Part I (A), General Report

The rural-rural migration in a district is highly and positively correlated with urban-rural migration and births per thousand population, moderately and positively correlated with rural-urban migration, literacy, and population depending on agricultural wages. Other variables, like density per square mile (negatively) percentage in agricultural occupation (negatively), gross production per acre (positively) are weakly correlated. Partial R-squares shows that the influence of density per square mile and acres won twice increases when other variables are controlled, and births per thousand shows a decrease (Table 4.7). Other variables lose their significance.

TABLE 32: Partial R-squares

....	Density per square mile	Literate in the district	Births per thousand	% in agricultural occupation	Per acre food grains production	Area sown twice as a % to net area cropped	Population dependent in agricultural wages
% of non-migrants in the district	0.283	0.511	0.075	0.056	0.046	0.042	0.042
% of intra-district rural to rural migrants	0.429	0.080	0.420	0.090	0.019	0.718	0.011
% of intra-district rural to urban migrants	0.159	0.036	0.178	0.008	0.013	0.008	0.086
% of intra-district urban to rural migrants	0.310	0.157	0.478	0.013	0.026	0.096	0.000
% of intra-district urban to urban migrants	0.353	0.000	0.244	0.397	0.076	0.523	0.048

All the correlations are lesser in magnitude in case of rural to urban migration. Literacy and births per thousand and rural migration and moderately and positively correlated with rural-urban migration. Variation in the rural to urban migration is least accounted for by chosen variables are partialized out on others. Urban-urban migration is highly correlated with percentage in agricultural occupations (negatively) and rural urban migration (positively). Among other variables correlated with it, density and percentage of literates are worth mentioning and both areas positively correlated. The area sown twice as a percentage of net area cropped show considerable explanatory power when other variables are controlled. But when the same is partial led out on other migration variables it loses its significance. Density per square mile and per cent in agricultural occupation shows an increase.

Overall density per square mile, literacy, births per thousand are important variables in understanding the variance in all types of migration. The chosen variables account for 86% of variation in the sedentary population in a district. The explanatory capacity of these variables is at its maximum (90%, Table 4.9) in rural-to-rural migration and at its minimum 61%, Table 4.8) in case of rural to urban migration. Since most of the variables used in analysis are agrarian in nature, this is to be expected.

The correlation analysis of different types of intra-district migration and other variables shows that the proportion of non-migrants in a district are moderately and negatively correlated with literates in a district and primary sector occupations. About 90% of variance in rural-to-rural migration in a district is accounted for by the chosen variables. Density per square mile, literacy, births per thousand population are important variables in understanding all types of migration. The rural to urban migration is least explained by the variables considered since the variables used in the analysis are agrarian in nature. Urban to rural migration, because of its high correlations with all other types of migration in a district, could be used as a maker.

TABLE 33: R-squares and R-bar-squares of different migration types in a district

		R-square	R-bar-square
1	Sedentary population in a district	0.86	0.76
2	Rural to rural migration in a district	0.90	0.84
3	Rural to urban migration in a district	0.61	0.36
4	Urban to rural migration in a district	0.80	0.67
5	Urban to urban migration in a district	0.77	0.62

Note: Six variables are used in the calculations namely (in a district): (1) Density; (2) Literacy; (3) Births per thousand population; (4) Percentage in agricultural occupations; (5) Gross production and food grains per acre; (6) Percentage of people dependent on agricultural wages

TABLE 34: Proportion of "locally born" persons and its sex ratio in state and districts

	Proportion of locally born persons			Sex ratio of locally born persons (F/Mx1000)	
	Total	Rural	Urban	Total	Rural
1	2	3	4	5	6
Bangalore	62.50	73.24	58.40	772	687
Belgaum	68.79	69.89	63.75	687	664
Bellary	70.59	73.54	60.47	794	776
Bidar	72.98	72.72	74.82	666	637
Bijapur	65.87	66.51	62.18	719	702
Chickmagalur	58.81	69.29	56.11	757	744
Chitradurga	70.53	73.53	56.30	741	721
Coorg	50.95	52.22	42.61	790	776
Dharwad	64.90	66.09	61.82	743	712
Gulbarga	70.15	70.88	66.34	691	663
Hassan	68.82	70.58	55.93	705	695
Kolar	71.30	72.85	66.00	709	676
Mandya	71.02	72.81	56.74	695	687

Mysore	74.33	75.09	69.00	752	724
North Kanara	59.44	60.07	56.45	788	763
Raichur	71.61	71.91	69.29	741	729
Shimoga	57.70	63.35	41.30	767	745
South Kanara	67.53	67.56	67.43	763	954
Tumkur	71.31	72.53	60.47	675	666
STATE	67.79	69.75	60.97	742	716

TABLE 35: Proportion of "locally born" persons and its sex ratio by R/U in state and districts—1971

	Proportion of locally born persons			Sex ratio of locally born persons (F/Mx1000)	
	Total	Rural	Urban	Total	Rural
1	2	3	4	5	6
Bangalore	66.92	71.02	63.63	813	718
Belgaum	67.39	68.76	62.11	685	664
Bellary	71.27	71.97	69.43	781	750
Bidar	73.53	73.37	74.39	637	608
Bijapur	66.95	67.86	56.96	733	714
Chickmagalur	62.91	63.76	58.27	775	767
Chitradurga	70.29	73.16	58.96	764	738
Coorg	56.14	57.64	47.94	816	804
Dharwad	64.81	65.75	62.75	756	722
Gulbarga	72.96	73.57	70.13	695	667
Hassan	70.61	72.52	58.58	702	687
Kolar	73.19	74.47	68.29	694	661
Mandya	72.55	74.82	58.33	712	702
Mysore	72.92	77.01	68.79	752	716
North Kanara	61.23	62.40	55.80	797	775
Raichur	71.79	70.82	70.68	767	750
Shimoga	60.45	62.44	54.02	779	752
South Kanara	68.82	68.95	68.31	953	946
Tumkur	70.56	72.19	58.23	695	681
STATE	68.74	70.31	63.85	752	721

INTERNAL MIGRATION AND POPULATION REDISTRIBUTION IN INDIA

This section examines the impact on the redistribution of population based on internal migration based on the data of preceding 19971 census. This redistribution does not explain in true sense the quantum and characteristics at various points of time which usually help determining the real redistribution.1 However, it defines the directions and quantum in some significance as how the population has been displaced in the country. The main emphasis is the identification of characteristics mostly on the consideration of inter-district and intra-district displacements. Besides, a view is presented with the population shift to urban centers and agglomerations of population 100,000 and above leading to inter-state migration.

Migration composition and urban growth:

Most people are familiar with the important function of the level of migration as a determinant of urban-regional growth. The composition of migration streams is also interrelated with rural-urban and inter-urban growth differentials. We encounter this last idea in discussions of regional disparities, where we often read statements to the effect that migration contributes to a spiral of decline among some regions by drawing off the more productive segments of their populations. We should locate the role of migration within the context of a broader growth model; since it is only one of several relevant factors and is itself a response to growth differentials.

Chart-I presents a highly simplified scheme of interrelation among selected determinants of population growth differentials among regions. This chart shows the composition of migration as being but one of a network of interrelated growth determinants. In terms of the amount of growth variance it explains, it may be significantly less important than several of the factors mentioned in the chart;

but we believe it to be a necessary condition of the maintenance of regional economic structural difference, and in regional labor adjustments to economic structural changes (in an open system of regions). Though the interaction of the composition of migration with economic structure, the former influences (and is influenced by) economic growth differences. There is also a more indirect path of influence of migration composition of economic growth differences through the impact of the former on population growth differences.

Rural urban characteristics:

In rural and urban areas of the country, the movements are typically various due to differences in opportunities. In rural areas immigrants to total rural population is high mostly in most districts of Punjab, Haryana, Assam (16.01—24.00%), parts of North Bengal (10--24%), Maharashtra, Madhya Pradesh (10.01—16%) and Tripura. On contrary, low ratio of rural migrants are noticed mainly in the thickly populated zones of Bihar, Andhra Pradesh, Tamil Nadu and Rajasthan in large number of districts in particular to name a few states. The variations in life-time inter-state net migration rates in rural and urban areas can be seen from Tables.

Proportions in urban areas are quite different. Maharashtra being industrially in favorable position shows very high proportion of urban migrants (81.98%) to total in-migrants. Delhi and Chandigarh, being highly urbanized are responsible for more than 90% of such populations. West Bengal counting greatly on its Calcutta. Howrah complex and the industrial belt hardly account for 52.05% of urban migrants. Gujarat (73.51%) and Tamil Nadu (66.89%) comparatively show different situations.

CHART—I: Selected Determinants of growth differentials among a set of regions.

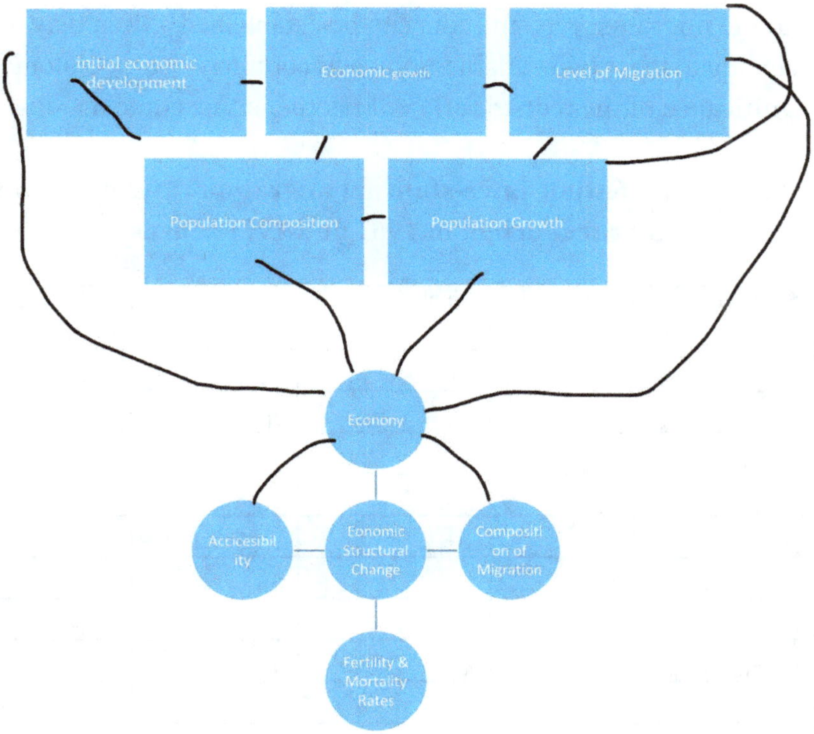

Note: Inside each box is the name given to a constellation of determinants. Arrows show the hypothesized major direction of influence between sets of determinants. Two headed arrows indicate major influence flowing in both directions. A given set of determinants is only partly influenced by another, and the former normally has substantial variation that is independent of other factors mentioned in the chart. Fertility and mortality rates would be a prime example of such “autonomous” variations.

Inter-district and intra-district patterns: A very important reflection of migrants is ruled out from the analysis of two variables, viz., intra-district (short distance) and inter-district (long distance) migration in the political frame of districts. If these two types are assessed further by supplementary rigorous field study data, probably more insight into the migration type in India can be established. Obviously, the mapping of these two variables indicates certain typical sociological significance of the redistribution of people in this context.

TABLE 36:Life-time inter-state net migration rates by sex and by rural/urban in 1961 and 1971 census

State/ Union Territories / India	Rural		
	Males		Females
	1961	1971	1961
Andhra Pradesh	-12.9	-11.1	-8.2
Assam and Meghalaya	34.5	27.0	17.5
Bihar	-45.3	-32.3	-15.4
Gujarat	-17.3	-13.5	-11.5
Jammu and Kashmir	-14.6	4.1	-4.7
Kerala	-21.6	-24.2	-5.5
Madhya Pradesh	6.4	5.2	4.8
Maharashtra	-1.9	-0.5	-2.3
Mysore	2.5	-1.7	0.4
Orissa	-19.0	-3.7	-6.0
Punjab Group	-37.2	-31.8	-21.4
Rajasthan	-27.7	-25.8	-20.6
Tamil Nadu	-23.5	-15.2	-19.2
Uttar Pradesh	-30.0	-30.7	-9.4
West Bengal	18.2	9.0	4.1
Delhi	75.9	198.5	56.9
Nagaland and Union Territories	26.9	33.5	21.6
ALL INDIA	-15.9	-13.2	-7.3

Note: Figures with minus sign indicates met out-migration rate.
Source: G.K. Mehrotra, Office of the Registrar General, India, Census of India, 1971, Series 1, India, Special Monograph No. 1, Birthplace Migration in India, 1974, Delhi.

TABLE 37:Life-time inter-state net migration rates by sex and by rural/urban in 1961 and 1971 census

State/ Union Territories / India	Urban		
	Males		Females
	1961	1971	1961
Andhra Pradesh	4.7	0.5	4.8
Assam and Meghalaya	134.6	125.5	28.5
Bihar	15.9	6.1	37.2
Gujarat	11.8	33.9	-5.7
Jammu and Kashmir	-33.3	-16.0	-22.8
Kerala	-98.9	-118.2	-53.8
Madhya Pradesh	124.6	107.2	88.7
Maharashtra	185.9	164.2	119.8
Mysore	47.7	20.2	35.9
Orissa	57.2	70.7	62.9
Punjab Group	-7.8	19.3	-31.4
Rajasthan	-23.5	-19.1	-19.0
Tamil Nadu	4.1	10.1	0.8
Uttar Pradesh	-27.1	-45.4	-8.7
West Bengal	208.5	125.6	80.6
Delhi	360.2	336.1	281.5
Nagaland and Union Territories	16.8	67.3	-22.5
ALL INDIA	70.0	54.9	37.5

Note: Figures with minus sign indicates met out-migration rate.
Source: G.K. Mehrotra, Office of the Registrar General, India,

Census of India, 1971, Series 1, India, Special Monograph No. 1, Birthplace Migration in India, 1974, Delhi.

Intra-district pattern: The evaluation of 357 districts of 1971 Census on intra-district movement indicates high proportion of females in rural and males in urban. Largely the contention is shifting females to husbands' house while in case of males various other accords may be established on this consideration. Probably, shifting of females after marriage from rural parents' house to rural husbands' house is more appropriate. On the contrary, intensity of female migration from rural house to urban is comparatively weak. This needs more probing. More important for any meaningful consideration is the movement of males in the intra-district migration. The predominance of female migration in rural areas to short distance movement besides marriage phenomena, a large proportion may belong to female agricultural labour. However, it is very clear that this type assists to be a greater extent in establishing class and seeks boundaries in the country on the basis of migration.

Inter-district pattern:

The movement of migrants from one district to another district of the same state/U.T. indicates a response to the variation in the economic development of the regions. If 25.01% and above is the limit of high movements in inter-district movement 20% parallel and 80o meridian from an enclave over India which retains high percentage of migrants resided in other districts of the state of enumeration to total migrants. This area falls mostly over Uttar Pradesh, Haryana, Punjab, Himachal Pradesh, Rajasthan, Gujarat, Madhya Pradesh, and Maharashtra. On the contrary, the entire eastern region comprising Bihar, West Bengal, Orissa, and Northeastern hill region below 20% is conspicuous. However, certain sporadic districts claim above 25% share in other areas in South India. In this type of movement, it is estimated that in the rural and urban sectors proportions of female migrants to total female migrants is higher. Similar trend is established in male migrants also. Probably in this type of movement family displacement may be ruled out.

Urban centers and agglomerations: The population of migrants in urban centers and agglomerations (100,000 and above) in the country is an indication of disparity between development and employment. If data is synthesized, the following characteristics are noted.

Extra-territorial and territorial:

(I) The feature more relevant is the distribution related to the partition of the country and its impact on socio-demographic relation of the past.2 The urban migrants if assessed according to place of birth, the migrants having place of birth outside India distributed mostly in the towns of north and western India. In this frame, maximum concentration of migrants is observed in the towns of Calcutta agglomerations, Delhi, Agartala, towns of Punjab, Haryana, Rajasthan, and Uttar Pradesh. Secondary concentrations are over Gujarat, Maharashtra, and Madhya Pradesh. A feeble concentration is also over Kerala and Tamil Nadu towns.

(ii) The other population category belonging to the territorial limits of India, i.e., whose last residence in other states but enumerated state (beyond the state of enumeration) is maximum (54.50) in Greater Bombay, Calcutta UA (44.45%), Delhi UA (74.78%) and Chandigarh (96.98%) to cite a few centers.

Economic status significance: The economic status attributes in this consideration is the working and non-working level with educational attainment of the migrants. The description is gloomy to a greater extent. If all the towns for which data are considered on functional basis, certain important issues emerge of the redistribution in urban agglomerations in the categories of poly-functional, bi-functional, and uni-functional centers. The poly-functional towns provide a comparatively diversified infrastructure to migrants for sustenance. Such infrastructures are very weak at such centers which have failed to display working and non-working proportions of migrants in the country. Since these centers are mostly located in the agricultural tracts whose articulation of development is not dynamic leave the migrants to under-development and unnourished. In this category, the non-working migrants represent higher proportions over working. Even, the port towns show this incidence to a greater degree.

Among the bi-functional towns, the structure of articulations is limited to either service, industry, or commerce. In this sector also, although the proportion of non-working migrants is comparatively higher than the working, the absorption of migrants according to educational levels in the working sector is low. At such centers the proportions of migrants having non-working status is very high.

Thirdly, the uni-functional centers in the country which are represented solely by either industrial or service in majority such as Calcutta, Bombay or steel towns or a few mining town provide a major base to migrants.

In this process of redistribution in urban areas, it may be remarked that the urban working migrants to total urban migrants lies mostly in the range of 35-60% in the country except Rajasthan and Uttar Pradesh where it is below 35%. In this social set-up migrants having primary and middle level education have large base of employment, followed by illiterates, matriculations, higher secondary, diploma, graduate and post-graduate and other technical degree personnel. The literates without educational level have their conspicuous share.

National perspective

A look on the 1961 and 1971 birthplace statistics at the national level indicates variations in female movement. Variation in urban sector stood at 21.47% in total in which female migration accounted for an increase of 25.25% as represented by Table 5.3. It is recognized that the rural sector being even, the urban was little modulated in the male and female sectors. If, in fact, undesirable effects of urban development have been experienced it may be worthwhile to reevaluate the nature of this development in male and female variations.

Again, across the borders of states in terms of gain and loss, the country illustrates five defined divisions of areas (Table 5.2). Here the total disparity in development is reflected in its manifold character both political and socio-economic. In strict sense, the developed states such as Maharashtra which was received about 52.16% net migrants being industrially rich (at least high in number of factories) indicates a progressive response to development attracting migrants. Others such as Punjab and Haryana being agriculturally developed (to some extent industrially) show less inward capability. Other areas such as Assam, Tripura, Delhi, and Chandigarh are the reflections of arrivals in high proportions on many socio-economic accords.

TABLE 38: India Migrants 1961 and 1971 Percent Variation.

Migrants (1961-71)	1961 and 1971 (Millions)			Per cent Variations	
	Total	Male	Female	Total	Male
Total	144.8 (166.7)	46.9 (53.7)	97.9 (113.50)	15.66	15.24
Rural	109.4 (123.4)	28.2 (31.7)	81.2 (92.2)	13.78	13.32
Urban	35.4 (42.8)	18.7 (22.0)	16.7 (20.8)	21.47	18.12

Source: D-II Table (Place of birth) 1961
D-I Table (Place of birth) 1971

Migration flow types and reflections: In this connection, the evaluation of a matrix on the basis of place of birth in the inter-state terms in four streams viz., (I) rural to rural, (ii) rural-urban, (iii) urban-urban, and (iv) urban-rural, if considered a considerable insight can be had in the developments.

(I) Rural to Rural : Flow especially of females is high from Karnataka to Andhra Pradesh (95 thousand) followed by Maharashtra to Andhra Pradesh (37 thousand), Tamil Nadu to Andhra Pradesh (34 thousand), from Uttar Pradesh to Madhya Pradesh (180 thousand), Punjab to Haryana (87 thousand), Delhi to Haryana (33 thousand) and Uttar Pradesh to Haryana (91 thousand). Flow of males from Bihar to Assam (112 thousand) is very high. Contribution of Uttar Pradesh and West Bengal to Assam in this is 24 and 20 thousand, respectively. Uttar Pradesh contributes males in Madhya Pradesh to the tune of 83 thousand which is sociologically important.

TABLE 39: Percentage net migration to gross migration

Receiving Area	Percentage Range	Losing Areas
Assam (77.51), Tripura (90.08), Andaman and Nicobar Island (91.99), Arunachal Pradesh (93.69), Chandigarh (80.88)	75.01 and above	
Maharashtra (52.16), Manipur (52.88), Meghalaya (59.49), Nagaland (74.96), West Bengal (74.96), Delhi (74.99), Lakshadweep (57.93)	50.01—75.00	Kerala (55.39)

Haryana (25.37), Madhya Pradesh (36.62), Sikkim (44.39), Dadar and Nagar haveli (40.26)	25.01—50.00	Bihar (30.34), Uttar Pradesh (32.87)
Gujarat (4.37), Jammu and Kashmir (16.06), Karnataka (2.91), Orissa (8.63), Punjab (16.55), Pondicherry (9.37)	25.00 and below	Andhra Pradesh (17.43), Himachal Pradesh (10.16), Rajasthan (9.97), Tamil nadu (5.56), Goa, Daman and Diu (5.14)

Source: Net Migration based on Table D-I (place of birth) of 1971 census.

1. A Mitra, Registrar General and Ex-Officio Census Commissioner for India, Census of India, 1961, Vol. I, India, Part II-C (ii), Migration Tables, D-II-Tables, India, 1966.

2. A Cahandra Sekhar, Registrar Genral and Census Commissioner, Census of India, 1971, Series I-India, Part II-D (i), Migration Tables (Tables D-I to D-IV); (D-II Tables, India, 1979).

(ii) Rural to Urban: Flow distribution among male is pronounced in general. In some characteristic cases Tamil Nadu to Andhra Pradesh (17,000 males), Karnataka to Andhra Pradesh (14,000), Kerala to Andhra Pradesh (11,000), Bihar to Assam (51,000), is the move followed by Uttar Pradesh to Assam (17,000), Bihar (55,000), highest being to Madhya Pradesh (110,000) and Maharashtra 333,000) males.

Female contribution in this direction is high from Gujarat to Maharashtra (147,000), Karnataka to Maharashtra (110,000), as examples.

(iii) Urban to Urban: Distribution is generally even both in males and females with narrow margins. Important trends lie between Gujarat to Maharashtra (128,000 males : 118,000 females) towards high balance. This is maintained in terms of Uttar Pradesh to Maharashtra, Karnataka to Maharashtra and Tamil Nadu to Maharashtra and Madhya Pradesh to Maharashtra. In some cases female migrants out-number males.

(iv) Urban to Rural: Urban to rural direction is generally weak. Significant contributors (above 10 thousand males and females) are Maharashtra to Gujarat, Tamil Nadu to Andhra Pradesh, Maharashtra to Madhya Pradesh, Uttar Pradesh to Madhya Pradesh, Maharashtra to Karnataka, Tamil Nadu to Karnatak and vice-versa and Keral to Tamil Nadu are notable.

These trends sectoral systems are geographically responsive. However, certain exceptions do occur.

Natural increase and migration

The migration system in the country is low which signifies some relation of economic development disparity and shift in population. The quantum of migration both inward and outward of 0-9 years duration is assessed in a particular state, an important indication is achieved to support the above view. The rise in population is due to natural increase where migration does not play a strong input (Table 5.5).

The depressed states in view of total development which are mostly losing in terms of inter-state migration show aptly inter-state position of out-migration high in absolute terms in Uttar Pradesh, Bihar, Kerala and Rajasthan where the components of natural increase is uniformly high. Taking into consideration the prosperous states of

Punjab and Haryana, it is interesting to find high out-migration and comparatively low inward flow in Punjab while Haryana is accounting for higher inward movement than outward. On the other hand, some industrially important states like Maharashtra, West Bengal, Gujarat, Delhi and Chandigarh show more arrivals indicating strong pull due to development at various locations and infrastructure.

TABLE 5.5: Percentage share of migration and natural increase to total variation, 1961-71

Gaining States										Losing States			
States/U.T.	Percentage of Share				States/U.T.	Percentage of share				States/U.T.	Percentage of Share		
	In	Out	Net	NI		In	Out	Net	NI		In	Out	Net
Assam	7	4	3	97	West Bengal	9	6	3	97	Andhra Pradesh	5	7	-2
Gujarat	7	6	1	99	Andaman & Nicobar Islands	45	7	38	62	Bihar	5	10	-5
Haryana	20	17	3	97	Arunachal Pradesh	22	4	18	82	Himachal Pradesh	16	19	-3
Madhya Pradesh	9	6	3	97	Chandigarh	94	22	72	28	Jammu and Kashmir	5	6	-1
Maharashtra	13	6	7	93	Dadra & Nagar haveli	40	11	29	71	Kerala	4	11	-7
Manipur	4	3	1	99	Delhi	58	17	41	59	Punjab	15	25	-10
Meghalaya	16	10	6	94	Lakshadweep	22	5	17	83	Rajasthan	8	11	-3
Mysore	10	9	1	99	Pondicherry	47	34	13	87	Tamil Nadu	6	7	-1
Nagaland	19	8	11	89	Goa, Daman & Diu	34	15	19	81	Tripura	5	5	-
Orissa	6	5	1	99						Uttar Pradesh	5	12	-7
Sikkim	15	11	4	96									

Source:

Table D-II, Migrants classified by place of last residence and duration of residence, 1971 census.

Abbreviations:

In : In-migrants ; Out: Out-migrants ; Net : Net Migrants-in-out ; NI : Natural Increase-Decadal variation-net migration (0-9 duration)

In this brief analysis, it is indicated that the study of redistribution in this context although presents some trends but does not direct towards the significance of migration/potentialities and economic development in the country. It is difficult to even quantify the share of migration due to economic reason.

The reflection which is obtained by the working, non-working and educational levels of migrants at urban centres to some extent indicate gaps between development and opportunities.

The parameters of study of internal movement need an overall consideration of developmental processes and communities and the level of responses and hence the data collection may demand micro synthesis. In this connection, it may be desirable to find out some way to assess the migration in households as this level is disintegrating both in rural and urban at the level of family system, religious and seeks; on the other hand, the agricultural and industrial relationships are difficult to articulate regional balance. It is essential to generate a system to study these with data so that at micro level redistribution can be established in long and short distances, within or through the points of geographic locations suitably divided in tiers to end from with economic inputs across the borders.

APPENDICES

Statement Showing Distribution Of Migrants (Figures In '00) By Different Age-Groups For Each State/Union Territory By Duration Of Residence 0-9 Years—1971 Census

Sex : Male

Age Group	Andhra Pradesh			Assam			Bihar			Gujarat			Haryana	
	I	O	I-O	I	O	I-O	I	O	I-O	I	O	I-O	I	O
0-2	81	83	-2	21	14	+7	47	59	-12	85	72	+13	73	59
3-7	217	242	-25	96	67	+29	183	300	-117	200	182	+18	208	231
8-12	186	249	-63	162	78	+84	198	483	-285	210	151	+59	231	225
13-17	130	184	-54	120	54	+66	117	383	-266	141	147	-6	208	171
18-22	244	328	-84	246	102	+144	199	887	-688	347	272	+75	311	269
23-27	255	356	-101	269	124	+145	224	827	-603	321	209	+112	282	215
28-32	240	294	-54	250	127	+123	250	791	-541	292	158	+134	264	184
33-37	140	221	-81	141	68	+73	181	446	-269	163	101	+62	138	128
38-42	136	161	-25	111	49	+62	126	353	-227	118	87	+31	112	100
43-47	77	96	-19	59	36	+23	70	156	-86	71	52	+19	52	51
48-52	77	69	+8	58	32	+26	50	130	-80	61	44	+17	60	64
53-57	47	27	+20	19	14	+5	37	49	-12	32	25	+7	31	31
58-62	29	39	-10	15	15	-	24	48	-24	26	34	-8	44	23
63-67	11	20	-9	3	7	-4	8	18	-10	11	9	+2	18	12
68-72	7	16	-9	8	4	+4	12	13	-1	14	9	+5	15	16
73+	12	6	+6	8	5	+3	13	15	-2	8	7	+1	16	17
Total	1889	2391	-502	1586	796	790	1739	4958	-3219	2100	1559	541	2063	1796

Note:

Figures are estimated on 1% sample basis.

O denotes Out-migrants

I denotes In-migrants.

I-O denotes Net migrants.

Statement showing distribution of migrants (figures in ’00) by different age-groups for each state/union territory by duration of residence 0-9 years—1971 census

Sex : Male

Age Group	Himachal Pradesh			Jammu & Kashmir			Kerala			Madhya Pradesh			Maharashtra	
	I	O	I-O	I	O	I-O	I	O	I-O	I	O	I-O	I	O
0-2	24	21	+3	32	12	+20	14	74	-60	80	73	+7	244	156
3-7	63	63	-	25	25	-	86	153	-67	335	240	+95	676	409
8-12	68	52	-16	26	16	+10	100	141	-41	422	228	+194	709	394
13-17	50	65	-15	24	24	-	73	164	-91	268	134	+134	615	217
18-22	71	147	-76	57	49	+8	131	492	-361	514	220	+294	1601	401
23-27	94	95	-1	72	87	-15	129	560	-431	488	240	+248	1442	381
28-32	79	111	-32	63	95	-32	139	387	-248	528	274	+254	1076	381
33-37	52	61	-9	26	46	-20	85	171	-86	308	145	+163	534	268
38-42	46	37	+9	21	26	-5	64	120	-56	194	136	+58	383	199
43-47	24	21	+3	7	15	-8	56	89	-33	113	79	+34	207	130
48-52	21	14	+7	7	15	-8	34	52	-18	114	72	+42	177	128
53-57	18	8	+10	1	1	-	18	22	-4	33	27	+6	76	55
58-62	6	8	-12	2	3	-1	14	28	-14	45	26	+19	61	63
63-67	2	5	-3	-	1	-1	12	12	-	28	9	+19	22	38
68-72	2	1	+1	2	2	-	3	6	-3	19	7	+12	20	22
73+	3	3	-	1	4	-3	2	7	-5	14	12	+2	24	12
Total	623	712	-89	366	421	-55	960	2478	-1518	3503	1922	+1581	7867	3254

Note:

Figures are estimated on 1% sample basis.

O denotes Out-migrants

I denotes In-migrants.

I-O denotes Net migrants.

Statement showing distribution of migrants (figures in '00) by different age-groups for each state/union territory by duration of residence 0-9 years—1971 census

Sex : Male

Age Group	Manipur			Meghalaya			Mysore			Nagaland			Orissa	
	I	O	I-O	I	O	I-O	I	O	I-O	I	O	I-O	I	O
0-2	1	-	+1	3	2	+1	87	98	-11	1	3	-2	47	14
3-7	2	2	-	20	7	+13	263	271	-8	6	1	+5	154	80
8-12	8	4	+4	18	12	+6	271	255	+16	3	4	-1	170	100
13-17	2	4	-2	13	8	+5	221	167	+54	9	1	+8	98	75
18-22	12	15	-3	38	11	+27	407	382	+25	61	8	+53	179	154
23-27	17	15	+2	32	28	+4	370	301	+69	64	17	+47	193	144
28-32	16	6	+10	24	17	+7	329	269	+60	41	14	+27	230	158
33-37	5	2	+3	14	7	+7	199	154	+45	19	6	+13	151	85
38-42	4	3	+1	12	10	+2	161	142	+19	14	4	+10	122	69
43-47	-	2	-2	6	7	-1	96	71	+25	9	2	+7	64	34
48-52	1	2	-1	3	4	-1	79	68	+11	4	3	+1	51	35
53-57	2	1	+1	1	2	-1	41	32	+9	-	1	-1	38	17
58-62	1	1	-	-	1	-1	55	37	+18	-	-	-	33	5
63-67	1	-	+1	-	-	-	27	11	+16	-	-	-	5	3
68-72	-	-	-	1	1	-	19	11	+8	-	1	-1	6	1
73+	1	-	+1	2	2	-	7	7	-	-	1	-1	5	3
Total	73	57		187	119	+68	2032	2276	+356	231	66	+166	1546	977

Note:

Figures are estimated on 1% sample basis.

O denotes Out-migrants

I denotes In-migrants.

I-O denotes Net migrants.

Statement showing distribution of migrants (figures in '00) by different age-groups for each state/union territory by duration of residence 0-9 years—1971 census

Sex : Male

Age	Punjab			Rajasthan			Tamil Nadu			Tripura			Uttar Pradesh	
Group	I	O	I-O	I	O	I-O	I	O	I-O	I	O	I-O	I	O
0-2	105	86	+19	41	120	-79	91	60	+31	2	2	-	60	211
3-7	285	276	+9	157	293	-136	227	253	-26	11	9	+2	213	609
8-12	251	322	-71	154	311	-157	185	239	-54	9	15	-6	278	799
13-17	182	262	-80	124	283	-159	147	188	-41	3	9	-6	177	753
18-22	320	396	-76	185	516	-331	266	373	-107	15	16	-1	346	1834
23-27	257	390	-133	149	407	-258	285	396	-111	16	17	-1	303	1737
28-32	224	348	-124	146	340	-194	237	385	-148	19	14	+5	299	1504
33-37	135	224	-89	97	182	-85	152	214	-62	6	6	-	167	719
38-42	108	173	-65	64	163	-99	125	194	-69	5	6	-1	155	504
43-47	58	101	-43	49	74	-25	82	111	-29	10	6	+4	74	264
48-52	50	97	-47	44	84	-40	73	99	-26	3	2	+1	69	211
53-57	22	49	-27	17	27	-10	24	52	-28	3	8	-5	35	96
58-62	24	55	-31	24	39	-15	34	40	-6	4	1	+3	42	90
63-67	6	23	-17	13	10	+3	17	24	-7	1	3	-2	23	34
68-72	13	16	-3	8	12	-4	12	16	-4	2	3	-1	13	36
73+	9	24	-15	12	15	-3	4	9	-5	-	1	-1	26	31
Total	2049	2842	-793	1284	2876	-1592	1961	2653	-692	109	118	-9	2280	9432

Note:

Figures are estimated on 1% sample basis.

O denotes Out-migrants

I denote In-migrants.

I-O denotes Net migrants.

Statement showing distribution of migrants (figures in '00) by different age-groups for each state/union territory by duration of residence 0-9 years—1971 census

Sex : Male

Age Group	West Bengal			Andaman & Nicobar Islands			Arunachal Pradesh			Chandigarh			Dadra & Nagar Haveli	
	I	O	I-O	I	O	I-O	I	O	I-O	I	O	I-O	I	O
0-2	57	60	-3	-	2	-2	3	-	+3	19	6	+13	1	-
3-7	246	224	+22	9	3	+6	8	2	+6	74	28	+46	3	5
8-12	380	240	+140	10	40	-30	4	2	+2	71	15	+56	1	1
13-17	368	185	+183	7	2	+5	3	3	-	61	17	+44	2	-
18-22	734	280	+454	29	1	+28	21	3	+18	127	21	+106	3	2
23-27	786	325	+461	51	2	+49	25	5	+20	137	13	+122	4	-
28-32	799	333	+466	31	2	+29	21	7	+14	91	25	+66	2	1
33-37	432	225	+207	15	4	+11	9	5	+4	58	8	+50	2	-
38-42	341	163	+178	10	2	+8	9	6	+3	39	10	+29	2	-
43-47	157	105	+52	2	2	-	5	1	+4	21	3	+18	-	1
48-52	140	96	+44	6	2	+4	5	-	+5	18	2	+16	2	-
53-57	46	58	-12	4	3	+1	1	-	+1	15	2	+13	-	1
58-62	47	31	+16	1	-	+1	2	-	+1	7	4	+3	-	1
63-67	18	15	+3	-	-	-	-	-	-	3	-	+3	1	-
68-72	10	12	-2	-	1	-1	-	-	-	4	1	+3	-	-

73+	14	20	-6	-	-	-	-	-	-	3	3	-	-	-
Total	4575	2372	+2203	175	66	109	116	34	82	746	158	588	23	12

Note:

Figures are estimated on 1% sample basis.

O denotes Out-migrants

I denotes In-migrants.

I-O denotes Net migrants.

Statement showing distribution of migrants (figures in '00) by different age-groups for each state/union territory by duration of residence 0-9 years—1971 census

Sex : Male

Age Group	Delhi			Goa, Daman and Diu			Lakshadweep			Pondicherry	
	I	O	I-O	I	O	I-O	I	O	I-O	I	O
0-2	98	35	+63	22	5	+17	-	-	-	3	15
3-7	321	124	+197	33	16	+17	-	-	-	22	28
8-12	407	138	+269	37	9	+28	-	-	-	19	15
13-17	393	82	+311	28	8	+20	-	-	-	15	9
18-22	794	126	+668	76	38	+38	3	2	+1	19	11
23-27	665	116	+549	73	33	+40	2	-	+2	26	9
28-32	596	124	+472	69	20	+49	-	1	-1	26	11
33-37	311	75	+236	38	10	+28	-	1	-1	15	11
38-42	275	65	+210	30	10	+20	2	-	+2	12	9
43-47	169	36	+133	8	6	+2	-	-	-	8	4
48-52	149	42	+107	15	4	+11	-	-	-	9	9
53-57	69	22	+47	5	6	-1	-	-	-	2	1
58-62	61	17	+44	11	-	+11	-	-	-	2	6
63-67	23	9	+14	10	-	+10	-	-	-	1	1

68-72	25	9	+16	4	2	+2	-	-	-	1	2
73+	30	10	+20	2	2	-	-	-	-	-	-
Total	4386	1030	3356	461	169	292	7	4	3	180	141

Note:

Figures are estimated on 1% sample basis.

O denotes Out-migrants

I denotes In-migrants.

I-O denotes Net migrants.

Statement showing distribution of migrants (figures in '00) by different age-groups for each state/union territory by duration of residence 0-9 years—1971 census

Sex : Female

Age Group	Andhra Pradesh			Assam			Bihar			Gujarat			Haryana	
	I	O	I-O	I	O	I-O	I	O	I-O	I	O	I-O	I	O
0-2	77	75	+2	15	21	-6	45	70	-25	84	59	+25	89	68
3-7	220	233	-13	86	67	+19	148	280	-132	208	184	+24	192	175
8-12	216	252	-36	111	74	+37	145	289	-144	151	165	-14	241	193
13-17	204	234	-30	62	64	-2	230	287	-57	124	118	+6	263	241
18-22	515	579	-64	138	106	+32	541	794	-253	375	300	+75	647	533
23-27	301	387	-86	131	77	+54	374	592	-218	299	294	+5	412	362
28-32	176	194	-18	102	64	+38	187	341	-154	179	169	+10	155	151
33-37	79	117	-38	43	23	+20	81	147	-66	61	62	-1	88	75
38-42	78	74	+4	31	23	+8	75	103	-28	61	49	+12	71	45
43-47	44	39	+5	18	17	+1	32	42	-10	37	34	+3	41	41
48-52	39	50	-11	17	8	+9	36	53	-17	25	36	-11	32	32
53-57	16	24	-8	8	9	-1	15	30	-15	19	15	+4	13	17
58-62	25	36	-11	12	6	+6	10	40	-30	31	19	+12	21	17

63-67	6	25	-19	11	7	+4	7	13	-6	11	14	-3	8	9
68-72	9	11	-2	5	4	+1	11	16	-5	13	10	+3	4	10
73+	9	8	+1	4	3	+1	6	7	-1	6	12	-6	15	13
Total	2014	2338	-324	794	573	221	1943	3104	1161	1684	1540	144	2292	1982

Note:

Figures are estimated on 1% sample basis.

O denotes Out-migrants

I denotes In-migrants.

I-O denotes Net migrants.

Statement showing distribution of migrants (figures in '00) by different age-groups for each state/union territory by duration of residence 0-9 years—1971 census

Sex : Female

Age Group	Himachal Pradesh			Jammu & Kashmir			Kerala			Madhya Pradesh			Maharashtra	
	I	O	I-O	I	O	I-O	I	O	I-O	I	O	I-O	I	O
0-2	24	23	+1	6	8	-2	36	71	-35	77	84	-7	229	142
3-7	51	36	+15	20	22	-2	75	142	-67	333	202	+131	621	392
8-12	41	51	-10	15	23	-8	102	128	-26	376	230	+146	575	339
13-17	31	26	+5	13	13	-	67	114	-47	376	293	+83	434	330
18-22	82	102	-20	49	38	+11	122	359	-237	1034	685	+349	1161	668
23-27	88	95	-7	46	25	+21	131	381	-250	628	380	+248	1012	588
28-32	44	30	+14	17	15	+2	65	175	-110	318	204	+114	555	334
33-37	20	24	-4	12	12	-	61	60	+1	176	100	+76	262	149
38-42	11	18	-7	6	6	-	28	56	-28	124	78	+46	175	124
43-47	5	14	-9	5	2	+3	26	34	-8	82	51	+31	102	81
48-52	4	8	-4	3	5	-2	24	39	-15	69	28	+41	109	53
53-57	4	3	+1	-	4	-4	10	16	-6	33	29	+4	63	36

58-62	1	2	-1	1	3	-2	10	20	-10	44	31	+13	74	40
63-67	-	1	-1	-	-	-	6	12	-6	26	17	+9	40	23
68-72	1	3	-2	-	1	-1	4	8	-4	21	16	+5	25	25
73+	2	3	-1	-	1	-	2	5	-3	13	8	+5	27	21
Total	409	439	-30	193	178	15	769	1620	851	3730	2436	1294	5464	3262

Note:

Figures are estimated on 1% sample basis.

O denotes Out-migrants

I denotes In-migrants.

I-O denotes Net migrants.

Statement showing distribution of migrants (figures in '00) by different age-groups for each state/union territory by duration of residence 0-9 years—1971 census

Sex : Female

Age Group	Manipur			Meghalaya			Mysore			Nagaland			Orissa	
	I	O	I-O	I	O	I-O	I	O	I-O	I	O	I-O	I	O
0-2	-	-	-	5	1	+4	82	115	-33	1	3	-2	54	13
3-7	3	3	-	15	11	+4	273	261	+12	8	2	+6	134	92
8-12	6	4	+2	12	9	+3	280	271	+9	6	8	-2	167	78
13-17	4	3	+1	14	6	+8	254	259	-5	6	2	+4	145	76
18-22	11	7	+4	31	15	+16	612	570	+42	10	7	+3	365	234
23-27	6	4	+2	23	7	+16	389	408	-19	12	-	+12	280	134
28-32	3	4	-1	15	10	+5	252	228	+24	8	1	+7	145	74
33-37	-	2	-2	5	3	+2	113	104	+9	1	-	+1	78	44
38-42	3	1	+2	5	4	+1	84	78	+14	1	2	-1	56	24

43-47	3	-	+3	2	4	-2	49	49	-	1	1	-	38	18
48-52	-	5	-5	-	7	-7	54	52	+2	-	1	-1	22	13
53-57	-	2	-2	3	1	+2	32	24	+8	1	-	+1	17	6
58-62	2	1	+1	2	1	+1	35	33	+2	-	-	-	27	7
63-67	1	-	+1	4	2	+2	25	9	+16	-	1	-1	5	4
68-72	-	-	-	-	1	-1	17	6	+11	-	-	-	11	2
73+	1	-	+1	1	1	-	16	8	+8	-	-	-	10	3
Total	43	36	7	137	83	54	2567	2467	100	55	28	27	1538	822

Note:

Figures are estimated on 1% sample basis.

O denotes Out-migrants

I denotes In-migrants.

I-O denotes Net migrants.

Statement showing distribution of migrants (figures in '00) by different age-groups for each state/union territory by duration of residence 0-9 years—1971 census

Sex : Female

Age Group	Punjab			Rajasthan			Tamil Nadu			Tripura			Uttar Pradesh	
	I	O	I-O	I	O	I-O	I	O	I-O	I	O	I-O	I	O
0-2	100	93	+7	57	101	-44	96	85	+11	1	1	-	81	207
3-7	196	232	-36	146	273	-127	191	231	-40	3	18	-15	196	549
8-12	201	273	-72	146	295	-149	152	258	-106	11	9	+2	234	543
13-17	168	254	-86	222	267	-45	161	189	-28	8	5	+3	316	509
18-22	460	595	-135	472	808	-336	387	510	-123	11	11	-	860	1611
23-27	320	489	-169	284	450	-166	343	426	-83	10	10	-	495	1145
28-32	163	222	-59	139	223	-84	195	244	-49	12	10	-2	221	646
33-37	61	145	-84	56	96	-40	99	134	-35	2	4	-2	133	289

38-42	48	91	-43	40	87	-47	67	105	-38	2	5	-3	77	194
43-47	30	49	-19	24	55	-31	49	67	-18	-	3	-3	49	100
48-52	31	50	-19	35	40	-5	31	55	-24	3	1	+2	38	101
53-57	12	31	-19	15	19	-4	20	36	-16	1	1	-	28	54
58-62	10	33	-23	18	35	-17	24	40	-16	-	2	-2	31	49
63-67	3	12	-9	8	12	-4	13	12	+1	1	1	-	11	25
68-72	9	13	-4	5	13	-8	8	15	-7	1	2	-1	19	26
73+	13	27	-14	6	9	-3	6	16	-10	1	-	+1	13	24
Total	1825	2609	-784	1673	2783	-1110	1842	2423	-581	67		-16	2802	6072

Note:

Figures are estimated on 1% sample basis.

O denotes Out-migrants

I denotes In-migrants.

I-O denotes Net migrants.

Statement showing distribution of migrants (figures in '00) by different age-groups for each state/union territory by duration of residence 0-9 years—1971 census

Sex : Female

Age Group	West Bengal			Andaman & Nicobar Islands			Arunachal Pradesh			Chandigarh			Dadra & Nagar Haveli	
	I	O	I-O	I	O	I-O	I	O	I-O	I	O	I-O	I	O
0-2	58	68	-10	1	2	-1	4	-	+4	28	11	+17	3	-
3-7	243	225	+18	5	3	+2	17	3	+14	58	17	+41	4	1
8-12	258	251	+7	7	2	+5	7	1	+6	47	18	+29	5	1
13-17	243	290	-47	2	5	-3	6	3	+3	49	14	+35	6	1
18-22	584	513	+71	9	1	+8	13	1	+12	93	24	+69	16	5
23-27	413	348	+65	13	3	+10	9	3	+6	77	18	+59	7	2

28-32	272	201	+71	8	2	+6	4	2	+2	51	15	+36	1	1
33-37	109	111	-2	3	4	-1	4	1	+3	22	7	+15	3	1
38-42	79	86	-7	4	-	+4	3	-	+3	17	10	+7	3	1
43-47	39	48	-9	3	-	+3	2	-	+2	12	1	+11	-	1
48-52	36	38	-2	1	2	-1	2	-	+2	11	2	+9	-	-
53-57	28	25	+3	-	-	-	-	-	-	7	1	+6	-	1
58-62	21	24	-3	-	-	-	-	-	-	7	1	+6	-	1
63-67	13	13	-	-	-	-	-	-	-	1	-	+1	-	-
68-72	15	12	+3	-	1	-1	-	-	-	2	1	+1	1	-
73+	6	13	-7	-	-	-	-	-	-	5	1	+4	-	-
Total	2417	2266	151	56	25	31	71	14	57	487	141	+346	49	16

Note:

Figures are estimated on 1% sample basis.

O denotes Out-migrants

I denotes In-migrants.

I-O denotes Net migrants.

Statement showing distribution of migrants (figures in '00) by different age-groups for each state/union territory by duration of residence 0-9 years—1971 census

Sex : Female

Age Group	Delhi			Goa, Daman & Diu			Lakshadweep			Pondicherry	
	I	O	I-O	I	O	I-O	I	O	I-O	I	O
0-2	112	54	+58	19	3	+16	-	-	-	6	12
3-7	312	111	+201	30	15	+19	2	-	+2	16	16
8-12	335	130	+205	48	19	+29	-	-	-	28	9
13-17	278	108	+170	35	15	+20	-	-	-	19	14
18-22	718	265	+453	48	39	+9	-	-	-	71	55

23-27	596	199	+397	63	34	+29	1	1	-	60	41
28-32	359	105	+254	31	20	+11	-	-	-	20	15
33-37	176	42	+134	27	15	+12	-	-	-	10	6
38-42	134	37	+97	14	4	+10	-	-	-	11	11
43-47	86	22	+64	5	3	+2	-	-	-	2	2
48-52	57	12	+45	13	2	+11	-	-	-	3	2
53-57	38	7	+31	9	5	+4	-	-	-	9	3
58-62	48	12	+36	4	3	+1	-	-	-	3	5
63-67	15	3	+12	2	1	+1	-	-	-	2	3
68-72	19	4	+15	1	3	+2	-	-	-	2	-
73+	26	5	+21	3	2	+1	-	-	-	1	2
Total	3309	1116	2193	352	183	169	3	1	+2	263	196

Note:

Figures are estimated on 1% sample basis.

O denotes Out-migrants

I denotes In-migrants.

I-O denotes Net migrants.

REFERENCES

Kundu, A. 2011a. Method in Madness: Urban Data from 2011 Census. Economic and Political weekly, Vol. 66(40), pp. 13-16.

1. (i) Census of India, Geographic Distribution of Internal Migration in India, New Delhi, 1980 (Directions B.K. Roy and Gen. Directions P. Padmanabha)

(ii) B.K. Roy, "Internal Migration in India's Manpower Resources", Net Geog. J. India, Vol. 25 (1), 1978.

(iii) B.K. Roy, "Internal Migration in India—An Evaluation of 1971 Census Data", Trans. Inst. Ind. Geog., Vol. 2(1), 1980.

2. ILO, International Migration, 1945-1957, Geneva, 1959 pp. 108-117.

3. Census of India, 'Geographic Distribution of Internal Migration in India', op. cit., pp. 9-10 and Map No.9.

4. Consult for such identifications in the census of India census Atlas (National Volume), 1971, Plate 40.

5. B.K.Roy, 'Potentiality of Environs of Growth Centers in India', in Balanced Regional Development, Oxford and IBH, Calcutta, 1971, pp. 66-71.

www.ingramcontent.com/pod-product-compliance
Lightning Source LLC
LaVergne TN
LVHW022053200926
848481LV00003B/896